T]

53,59,

NOTES

including
- *Biographies*
- *Historical Background*
- *Summaries and Commentaries*
- *Review Questions*
- *Selected Bibliography*

by
George F. Willison
Formerly Director of Public Information,
*   United Nations*
Author of Patrick Henry and His World

Cliffs Notes

INCORPORATED

LINCOLN, NEBRASKA   68501

Editor	Consulting Editor
Gary Carey, M.A. *University of Colorado*	*James L. Roberts, Ph.D.* *Department of English* *University of Nebraska*

Cliffs Notes, Inc.   Lincoln, Nebraska

CONTENTS

The Federalist Notes

BIOGRAPHIES

On October 27, 1787, the first of a long series of articles on the proposed new federal constitution appeared in the New York City press. The first seven articles were published in the columns of the *Independent Journal*. Later, other essays in the series appeared in the *New York Packet* and the *Daily Advertiser*.

The articles were, for the most part, rather short because of limitations of space in the small newspapers of the day. All of them were in essay form, political in subject matter, and quite frankly partisan in spirit and purpose. They were designed to mobilize public opinion in support of the new national constitution proposed by the Constitutional Convention that had met in Philadelphia from late May to mid-September, 1787.

That convention, after long and often very acrimonious debate, had finally agreed to a plan for setting up a whole new governmental framework for the country, and had ordered that the proposal be submitted to the thirteen states for ratification or rejection.

Throughout the country, from New England to Georgia, responsible public opinion was sharply divided on the merits of the scheme. For one thing, it entailed the complete scrapping of the Articles of Confederation under which Americans had successfully concluded the Revolution. A great many persons questioned the rush for a change.

The articles in the New York press urging quick ratification of the proposed new scheme of things were put together and, with eight more essays added, hurriedly published in book form as *The Federalist,* in two small volumes. All the newspaper articles, and the book as well, bore the signature of one "Publius" as author.

It soon transpired that "Publius" was 51 parts Alexander Hamilton, 29 parts James Madison, and five parts John Jay. The authors will be discussed in that order.

ALEXANDER HAMILTON

Born on the tiny island of Nevis, in the British West Indies, Alexander Hamilton (1757-1804) was a "natural" child, a curious but popular euphemism of the day, meaning that he was a bastard, born out of wedlock, the son of a Scottish merchant, James Hamilton, a man of good family but rather indolent and of little business ability. His common-law wife was Rachel Faucette, a rather well-to-do Creole of French Huguenot descent who had married a Dane and had long been separated from him. The law, however, blocked her from obtaining a divorce and remarrying. She and Hamilton had two sons, Alexander being the elder.

In later years, Hamilton's political and personal enemies made a number of remarks about Hamilton's illegitimacy. After a harsh quarrel, John Adams called him the "bastard brat of a Scots pedlar." Jefferson jibed at him as "that foreign bastard." An influential writer-editor-publisher of the day, James Callender, referred to him often as the "son of a camp girl." Such remarks were obviously unfair, and unworthy of those who made them.

In 1772, after the death of his mother and his father's bankruptcy, young Alexander, at the age of fifteen, was sent by Faucette relatives and family friends to the mainland to continue his education. Landing at Boston, Hamilton went to New Jersey to finish his preparatory studies and, in 1774, moved to New York City to enroll in King's College (a Church of England institution), soon renamed Columbia College, the original unit of Columbia University.

It was a time of crisis and confusion. The conflict between Britain and the thirteen colonies, long simmering, was coming to a boil and soon erupted into open hostilities after the clash of arms at Lexington and Concord. Young Hamilton, throughout his life a supporter of legally constituted authority, was at first inclined to be pro-British in his views and sympathies.

But he soon changed his mind, not because he subscribed to the then radical doctrines of Jefferson, Patrick Henry, Tom Paine, Sam Adams, George Mason, and other revolutionary democrats. And even more, not because he approved of the often riotous proceedings of the Sons of Liberty, who could be very rough on their Tory adversaries, most of them men of substantial property. Many of these Tories were tarred and feathered, or worse.

Hamilton always had the highest regard for property, and particularly for men who owned large quantities of it. He embraced the cause of the patriots (or "rebel scoundrels," as King George III termed them) because he had become a nationalist, swinging to the view that separation of the colonies from the mother country was not only inevitable, but desirable.

With characteristic boldness and energy, young Hamilton, still a collegian, organized a militia company and was elected captain. This was an artillery company, the self-styled "Hearts of Oak," whose bravery and military proficiency soon came to the attention of Gen. George Washington, commander-in-chief of Continental forces since June, 1775. The general was so impressed that, early in 1777, he made Hamilton a lieutenant colonel and called him to become his private secretary and confidential aide, a very responsible post for a youth just turned twenty.

For four years Hamilton served brilliantly at that post, being at Washington's side during the awful winter of 1777-78 at Valley Forge and down to the culminating American victory at Yorktown where Hamilton, now a full colonel, led an assault that captured the key British redoubt.

Meanwhile, in 1780, Hamilton had married Elizabeth Schuyler, a daughter of Gen. Philip Schuyler, thus becoming a member of a rich and influential New York family, closely related to the Van Rensselaers and other old Dutch patroon families with their vast landed estates along both banks of the Hudson and elsewhere. Hamilton was now well on his way up the social and financial ladder.

After the war, Hamilton resumed his studies, became a lawyer, and soon opened his own office. He had many clients, but being a man of vast ambition, he found the routines of a private law practice not very challenging. They did not begin to use up his driving physical energy or satisfy his broad intellectual interests. More and more, he immersed himself in politics and public affairs. As one of New York's delegation to the 1782-83 session of the Continental Congress, he saw for himself, to his dismay, the many weaknesses and disabilities of the national government under the Articles of Confederation.

Almost everyone agreed that the Articles should be amended to strengthen the powers and reform the procedures of the central government. But here agreement ended. Almost everyone — Washington,

Jefferson, Franklin, Patrick Henry, George Mason, John Adams, Sam Adams, Alexander Hamilton, James Madison, among many more — had his own notions about what an ideal constitution should contain. The notions privately entertained by Hamilton, which were extreme and almost incredibly authoritarian and politically simplistic, will be outlined later.

Hamilton made himself a leader in the movement to call a convention to consider revisions of the Articles of Confederation. Hamilton spoke for those who shared his view that the rights of property should be defended and secured above all else, that such rights provided the very foundation of society and orderly government, and that the existing government did not adequately protect such rights. To those holding these views the country was on the brink of disaster, especially because of fiscal and commercial problems.

But the people at large, and the highest authorities in most states, did not take this alarmist view. They did not see the nation facing any grave immediate crisis. Consequently, when the convention assembled at Annapolis in September, 1786, only five states were represented: New York, Pennsylvania, Virginia, New Jersey, and Delaware. As it was obvious that no business could be done under the circumstances, the twelve delegates chose Hamilton to draft an address calling on all the states to send representatives to a new constitutional convention to meet in Philadelphia early in May the next year.

On the day the Philadelphia convention was to open, not enough states were represented to constitute a quorum. Several weeks passed before a quorum of seven was present. Delegations from five more states later came in. One state, Rhode Island, did not send a delegation. Radical and agrarian in its general views, it regarded the convention as a trap devised by large landed proprietors and rich conservative urban families to advance their special interests, a view widely held in other states.

Sitting from late May to mid-September, 1787, the Philadelphia convention adopted a document, a patchwork of compromises and accommodations between many sharply conflicting points of view, and the Congress sent copies of the proposed constitution to the state legislatures, each of which was to call a special convention to adopt or reject the proposal.

For reasons to be discussed later, Hamilton did not like the proposed constitution. But he felt that anything was better than the Articles of Confederation, and threw his full energies into efforts to secure ratification of the Philadelphia document. His main effort went into contributions to the long series of newspaper articles published in book form as *The Federalist*. Hamilton conceived the idea of the series and, as noted before, wrote most of the argumentative essays, with Madison and John Jay contributing others.

The fight for and against ratification was bitter, particularly in the larger states. By the end of July, 1788, the proposed constitution had been ratified by eleven states, the last two being Virginia and New York. This was two more than the requisite number. If Virginia had declined to ratify — and the margin was slim, 88 votes for, 80 against — New York would have followed suit and not ratified, and Pennsylvania would no doubt have reversed its close vote of approval, obtained by force and duress. It was stipulated that if nine states ratified the constitution, it was to go into effect immediately. But if the three largest, richest, and most populous states — Virginia, New York, and Pennsylvania — declined to ratify, there can be no doubt that the proposed constitution would have been sent back to another national convention for revision and amendment.

The Congress adjourned and there was technically no federal government until the following March, when the newly elected Congress met at New York. Washington became the first president of the United States and, for the two most important posts in his administration, chose Jefferson as secretary of state and Hamilton as secretary of the treasury.

Hamilton took hold of the duties of office in his usual brisk manner. Early in 1790, he submitted his first report on the public credit. National credit was in dire straits. The report dealt specifically with the debts inherited from the Confederation, which were considerable in terms of the day. Foreign debts owed by the government amounted to some $12,000,000, and domestic debts to some $45,000,000. In addition, the states had Revolutionary War debts estimated at $25,000,000.

To maintain the public credit and build confidence at home and abroad in the new government, to strengthen it by fostering interest among the business groups holding most of the domestic debt, Hamilton proposed that national, foreign, and domestic debts be funded at par value, and that the federal government assume, up to some $21,500,000, the debts incurred by the states during the years of the American Revolution.

Funding of the foreign debt aroused little opposition, but the plan to fund domestic national debt was bitterly attacked since much of the currency and many of the bonds had been sold to speculators at high discount, and the speculators rather than the original holders would be the ones to profit when the currency and bonds were redeemed at face value. The attack on the proposal that the national government assume responsibility for the repayment of state debts of certain kinds met with even heavier opposition, and the division took place along sectional lines.

In general, the northern states, especially those in New England, had the largest unpaid debts and therefore favored assumption which would ease their tax burden by spreading it around. On the other hand, most southern states had made arrangements to clear their indebtedness and therefore objected to a measure that would greatly increase the national debt, for the servicing of which their inhabitants would be taxed.

Virginia took the lead in opposing the assumption measure. In strong resolutions drafted by Patrick Henry, Virginia protested that Hamilton's scheme would profit and maintain a monied interest, that agriculture would be subordinated to commercial and financial interests, that the proposal would undermine republican institutions, and that there was "no clause in the Constitution authorizing Congress to assume the debts of states."

When the assumption bill came to its first vote in the House of Representatives, it was defeated. But Hamilton, never daunted, was not prepared to give up. He would make a deal. Meeting Madison at a dinner party arranged by Jefferson, he made a proposition: he would use his utmost influence to gather enough northern votes to assure that the national capital would be established along the Potomac, a step that should placate the southerners. In return, Madison should do his best to get enough southern votes to assure the adoption of the assumption measure.

Thus, instead of going to Philadelphia or New York, the largest cities, the national capital went south to the Potomac, to the District of Columbia, a ten-mile-square unsettled tract, not yet chosen, and where a city had yet to be built. In a real sense, Hamilton was the founder of Washington, D.C.

In his next bold step Hamilton proposed the chartering of a bank to be owned and operated by the national government, the Bank of the

United States. When consulted about this by President Washington, Secretary of State Jefferson forcefully declared his opinion that such a step was clearly unconstitutional. Taking a "strict constructionist" view of the Constitution, Jefferson declared that chartering of a national bank was not one of the powers delegated to Congress.

Taking a "loose constructionist" view of the Constitution, and developing for the first time the doctrine of "implied powers," Hamilton replied that the national government had been empowered to collect taxes and regulate trade, and that a national bank was an efficient and proper means of executing that power. Such a bank was not forbidden by any particular provision of the Constitution, and therefore "it may safely be deemed to come within the compass of the national authority."

President Washington wavered between Jefferson's view and that of Hamilton, finally taking Hamilton's, thereby following his practice of accepting the counsel of the cabinet officer most immediately concerned in any question at issue.

Dissension within the Washington administration about national policies became ever more pronounced, with one group led by Hamilton, and the opposing one by Jefferson. Our political party structure had its origins in the conflicts here.

Hamilton spoke for those who believed, as he did, that the national government should actively promote the development of manufacturing, commerce, banking, and shipping. Infant American industries should be protected from competition by erecting high tariff barriers against foreign imports. This would be not only good in itself, but incidentally would produce considerable revenues for the national government.

There should be the strongest possible central government under strong executive leadership. The reins of power should be kept as far as possible from popular control. The country should be governed by an elite group, which, as Hamilton defined it, was the propertied class. As men of property literally "owned" the country, their voice in public affairs should be, if not exclusive, at least always predominant.

Opposing such views, Jefferson led those who distrusted an overriding central government. There should be a minimum of industrialization, urbanism, and organized finance. Wealth should be broadly diffused, to lessen the gap between rich and poor. The ideal society was a democratic agrarian order based on the individual freeholder. The people, acting through their elected representatives, should be left to govern themselves. Jefferson believed they had the ability to do so. Those who shared Jefferson's views began organizing groups that soon coalesced nationally as the Democratic-Republican party, which strongly opposed the measures advocated by the Federalist party headed by Hamilton.

The split between Hamilton and Jefferson was widened by the impact of the French Revolution which was well on its way by that historic July 14, 1789, when Parisians razed the hated fortress-prison, the Bastille, which was to become the symbol of autocratic oppression. This revolution shook to its foundations the *ancien régime* with all its semi-feudal trappings in church and state. Crowned heads throughout Europe began to tremble, particularly after France declared herself a republic and sent King Louis XVI and Queen Marie Antoinette to the guillotine, and many titled aristocrats and rich *bourgeois* as well.

After many provocations and attempts at intervention by foreign powers, revolutionary France declared war on Britain, Spain, and Holland, the start of a war that went on almost continuously for twenty-two years, ending with Napoleon's defeat at Waterloo in 1815.

Though deploring its excesses, Jefferson remained very sympathetic toward revolutionary republican France. Favoring monarchy and an aristocratic order of things, Hamilton was strongly pro-British. But the two men agreed on one point, and the most important: the United States should not become involved in any way in the European war. Each had a hand in drafting the proclamation President Washington issued in 1793 annoucing American neutrality, though the word "neutrality" was not used.

In addition to other differences between Hamilton and Jefferson, a matter of personality was involved. Hamilton was always a difficult man to get along with, having a rather abrasive character. For one thing, he had no sense of humor, and took himself very seriously, which led him into many serious as well as silly quarrels that might well have been avoided. While he could be very charming when he pleased, he was often very arrogant, opinionated, and stubborn; and while not greedy or corrupt, he could be ruthless in advancing himself and the causes he favored.

Under President Washington, Hamilton began to attempt the functions of a prime minister on the British model. This very much annoyed Jefferson who, as secretary of state, held top rank and was *ex officio* the chief officer in the cabinet. But more than status was involved here. Jefferson and other cabinet officers were soon complaining that Hamilton, by his policies and practices as secretary of the treasury, was intruding into and interfering with the operations and decision-making of their departments as if he were, in fact, prime minister. At the end of 1793, Jefferson resigned as secretary of state, and issued a public blast against Hamilton, what he stood for, and what he was doing.

Hamilton was a danger to the country as constituted, said Jefferson. His fiscal system "flowed from principles adverse to liberty, ... and was calculated to undermine and demolish the republic." In a real sense, this was true. To the end of his life, Hamilton openly avowed his dislike of republicanism, which was exceeded only by his distrust of the people and what he called "open democracy."

Early in 1795, Hamilton resigned as secretary of the treasury and returned to New York City to resume his law practice there. But he remained a powerful political influence behind the scenes. When President Washington decided to step down after his second term in office, it was Hamilton who drafted most of the celebrated "Farewell Address."

Though out of public office, Hamilton was always ready with counsel and advice, but the new president, John Adams, was not as receptive to it as Washington had been. On receiving Hamilton's recommendation for a very aggressive anti-French, pro-British foreign policy, which would have meant instant war, Adams exclaimed: "This man is stark mad, or I am."

The president and Hamilton became estranged and soon violently quarreled, with Adams denouncing Hamilton as an "unprincipled intriguer." With the approach of the 1800 election, Adams wanted to continue as president and was furious when he discovered that Hamilton was working to defeat him by organizing Federalist support for another candidate.

The 1800 election resulted in a resounding Federalist defeat all along the line. The Democratic-Republicans had two presidential aspirants: Jefferson of Virginia (vice president under Adams) and Aaron Burr of New York City, a brilliant lawyer and an adroit political organizer and manipulator. It was Burr who put new life into the Society of St.

Tammany in New York City, transforming it from merely a social club into an overpowering political force, the notoriously corrupt Tammany Hall of later years.

When the electoral college met after the election, the vote to designate the president resulted in a tie: 73 votes for Jefferson, the same for Burr, with John Adams trailing at 65. The other Federalist candidate, Charles Cotesworth Pinckney, actively supported by Hamilton, ran close behind Adams with 64 votes. Thus Hamilton spiked President Adams' ambitions, and was to play an even more decisive role in choosing the next president. The tie vote in the electoral college threw the choice of a president to the House of Representatives, as the Constitution stipulated.

In the House, the balloting for the presidency went on and on, ballot after ballot. Finally, the Federalist members, after a caucus, decided to back Aaron Burr, but Hamilton objected. He and Burr had been rather close friends for years, but it appeared that from the start Hamilton had distrusted Burr and his intentions, describing him in his private correspondence as an "unprincipled and dangerous man." Hamilton disliked Jefferson and abhorred his Democratic-Republican principles, but he even more disliked what he regarded as Burr's blustering political opportunism. Concluding that Jefferson was the lesser of two evils, Hamilton swung the New York vote to Jefferson. On the thirty-sixth ballot, Jefferson became our third president, with Burr as vice president

Hamilton received no reward for his action in breaking the presidential deadlock. His influence under the Jefferson administration was nil. All he gained was what he regarded as a good conscience and the lasting animosity of his old friend Burr. It was not long before the two men clashed again, and bloodily. In 1804, Burr decided that he would like to be governor of New York and offered himself as a candidate. Hamilton immediately came out of semi-retirement and did his best to defeat him, which he accomplished. Burr turned on Hamilton, informing him that he had it on good authority, in a published letter, that Hamilton, in company, had spoken of him as "despicable, . . . a dangerous man, and one who ought not be trusted with the reins of government." Burr demanded "satisfaction" in accord with the gentlemen's code of honor of the time.

As Hamilton in his pride was not prepared to issue a flat disclaimer of what he was reported to have said in company at one time, for he had often spoken ill of Burr, a duel was arranged, to be fought on the Jersey side of the Hudson, opposite Manhattan, on the heights at Weehawken, a favorite ground for such encounters. The field on Weehawken Heights was a doubly tragic one for the Hamiltons. Their oldest son, Philip, had been killed there in a duel three years previously, in 1801, while still a student at Columbia College.

In the very early morning of July 11, 1804, Hamilton and Burr faced each other with pistols at twenty paces. At the signal, two shots rang out and Hamilton fell forward, gravely wounded, shot through the groin. Carried back across the river in the barge on which he had come over, he was taken to a friend's house in lower Manhattan where he died the next day, in his forty-seventh year, a premature and tragic end for one who was a great American, no matter what one may think of his political and social philosophy. And in historical perspective, it should not be forgotten that Hamiltonianism has been a strong, often dominant, tone in American public and private life since his day, though its echoes may now be fading.

Whatever his other qualities, Hamilton had a strong, incisive, logical mind, unquestioned courage, boundless energy, deep devotion to duty, and an unremitting zeal in forwarding the public good along the lines he thought best. He also possessed a masterful pen as an advocate for whatever cause he favored. As his bitter and eventually fatal enemy Burr once remarked, with awe and reluctant admiration, "Anyone who puts himself down on paper with Hamilton is lost."

JAMES MADISON

James Madison (1751-1836) became the fourth president of the United States, succeeding his close friend Jefferson. Madison was born on a large plantation in Virginia, the oldest of twelve children in a family that was, as Madison once observed, "not among the most wealthy in the country, but in independent and comfortable circumstances." Very studious from his youth, Madison attended the College of New Jersey (Princeton), and graduated in 1772, having centered his interests in history, law, and theology.

Madison first entered public life as a delegate elected to the Fourth Virginia Convention which met in Williamsburg in May, 1776, to deal with the developing revolutionary situation. As a novice among such older and more experienced patriot leaders as Patrick Henry, Richard Henry Lee, George Mason, and others, "young Jaimie," as friends called him, did not play much of a part in the decision-making. He was active and served effectively on several important committees in the historic Fourth Virginia Convention that declared Virginia's independence from Britain months before our national Declaration of Independence, framed a new constitution, and issued Virginia's celebrated Declaration of Rights. This later became the basis of our national Bill of Rights, the first ten amendments to our Constitution, laying down specifically the individual rights of citizens. The Virginia Declaration of Rights was largely the work of the great George Mason, though Patrick Henry and Madison may have had a hand in it. In any case, it was Madison who pushed twelve amendments through the first session of Congress under the new federal Constitution. Ten of these amendments were ratified in all the states by 1791; we know these as our Bill of Rights.

In 1776, Madison was elected to the House of Delegates, the lower house of the state legislature under Virginia's new constitution, but was defeated when he sought re-election. From 1779 through 1783, Madison was a member of the Virginia delegation to the Continental Congress where he saw and experienced, as Hamilton had, the difficulties of governing the country efficiently under the Continental Congress and the Articles of Confederation. He advocated the granting of additional powers to the Congress, and measures forbidding the states to issue any more paper money, which was depreciating rapidly and ruining public credit.

When his term in Congress ran out, Madison returned to Virginia and established a law practice, which did not much interest him. Again elected to the Virginia House of Delegates, he introduced and strongly supported Jefferson's bill to establish absolute religious freedom in the state, with complete separation of church and state.

With Maryland and Virginia in dispute about their boundaries and commercial rights along the Potomac, Madison proposed and arranged a meeting that amicably settled that dispute. This led Madison to think that all the states should be invited to send commissioners to a general conference to settle trade, commercial, and other conflicts among them. This led to the abortive convention at Annapolis in 1786 but this, in turn, with Madison and Hamilton energetically pushing, led to the successful Constitutional Convention at Philadelphia the following year.

At that convention Madison was perhaps the most active member, attending all sessions except for the few times when he was ill. Also, he was perhaps the most influential member, winning the salute of almost all as "father of the Constitution." He had read long, deep, and to good purpose in constitutional history and theory.

When the proposed new constitution came before the Virginia Constitutional Convention for ratification or rejection, the division of opinion in that crucial state was close and sharp. Madison, with his precise logic and wide knowledge, was its chief and ablest defender, but not its most eloquent. He was never a good public speaker: he had a squeaky and rather irritating voice. He had no skill to match the impassioned oratory of Patrick Henry, the leader of many eminent Virginians and Americans elsewhere who were resolutely opposed to immediate ratification and wanted the Philadelphia document sent back for revision before considering the final adoption. Also, as Madison was a short, frail man, being less than five feet six inches tall, he was not an impressive figure on the platform. In large halls, he could scarcely be seen over the lectern if it was high. On such occasions, Madison wore special shoes with very high heels to increase his physical stature.

In the first session of the United States House of Representatives, in addition to making the proposals that led to the adoption of the first ten amendments, Madison introduced resolutions for establishing the three main executive departments under the new government: foreign affairs, treasury, and war.

Though the two had been close allies at the Philadelphia convention and in writing the Federalist papers, Madison soon broke with Hamilton and the Federalists, joining the Democratic-Republican forces rallying around Jefferson. The break was occasioned by Madison's objections to Hamilton's fiscal policies. Madison agreed with Jefferson that these policies were deliberately designed to undermine the constitutional republican form of government, and because he felt that, under the influence of Hamilton's strong anti-French, pro-British views, the Federalist administration was assuming an "Anglified complexion" against the wishes of a popular majority sympathetic with France and French republicanism.

Madison retired from Congress in 1797. Nevertheless he remained very active in public life. Always a libertarian, he joined Jefferson and many others in denouncing and opposing the atrocious Alien and Sedition acts, passed in 1798 in the name of national defense and security. The real purpose was to suppress all criticism, especially published criticism, of the Federalist scheme of things and the incumbent administration's policies, foreign and domestic.

Many were fined or jailed, or both; many more were constantly harassed on the orders of authorities who regarded every dissenter as a foreign agent, a member of a vast international conspiracy. The Alien and Sedition acts, which caused a wide split throughout the country, were among the worst and most oppressive laws ever put on our books.

Against the harsh and repressive Alien and Sedition acts Madison drafted the strong Virginia Resolutions, and Jefferson the equally strong Kentucky Resolutions, adopted by the legislatures of those states. These resolutions declared that the national government was exceeding the powers delegated to it by the Constitution, that every state had "an equal right to judge for itself" infractions of the Constitution by the national government, and had not only the right but the duty "to interpose for arresting the progress of the evil."

This was very subversive indeed, laying a foundation for the doctrine of nullification that later led to the Civil War. But neither Madison nor Jefferson was hurt by the controversy, though many men of lesser influence who shared their views were prosecuted—and persecuted—by the Federalists. With public indignation against the Alien and Sedition acts mounting, Jefferson was elected president in 1800, and his Democratic-Republican party took command of the Congress, sending the Federalists down in a crushing defeat from which that party never recovered. It expired in the next decade.

In one of his first acts, President Jefferson granted amnesty to all those convicted under the Alien and Sedition laws, and persuaded Congress to indemnify those who had been ordered to pay fines under those laws, including interest on their fines.

Jefferson chose Madison as his secretary of state, and the two worked closely together for eight years. The direction of American foreign affairs presented formidable problems for the infant republic. With the Napoleonic Wars raging in Europe, Jefferson and Madison found it difficult to steer a safe course in very troubled waters, doing their best to keep the country from becoming involved with the belligerents on either side, in spite of annoying provocations by both sides.

Undoubtedly their greatest achievement was the acquisition of the Louisiana Purchase in 1803, for which the United States paid Napoleon some $15,000,000. This enormous tract, a vast but ill-defined territory, included some 830,000 square miles of land.

But the Federalists, swinging away from Hamilton's "loose construction" interpretation of the Constitution, now charged Jefferson, formerly a "strict constructionist," with stretching the Constitution too far and violating it. Jefferson was not authorized to acquire foreign territory by purchase. Besides, he was wasting the taxpayers' money in buying a ghastly wilderness.

On deciding to step down after two terms as president, following Washington's example, Jefferson pointed to Madison as the man he preferred to succeed him. Madison won easily, receiving 122 votes in the electoral college to his nearest rival's 47. More than twenty years before, in 1794, he had married Mrs. Dolley (Payne) Todd, a handsome, young, and wealthy widow, who won great admiration and a name for herself as "Dolly" Madison, one of the most charming first ladies ever to grace the White House.

Madison's two terms as president (1808-16) were very trying, both for him and for the country. In a disordered world, foreign complications continued to build up, particularly with the British and the French who were still at war. On the one hand, Britain continued to take a very high-handed course in its efforts to dominate the seas, capturing American ships charged with carrying "contraband" (as defined by the British), and taking sailors off American vessels and forcing them to serve in the Royal Navy and other services. On the other hand, the United States was having naval skirmishes with the equally high-handed French under Napoleon.

Matters came to a head after British warships increased their vigilance outside east coast harbors in 1811. On June 1, 1812, Madison sent a war message to Congress, and war was declared. Except for some American successes in isolated clashes at sea, the War of 1812 was a series of military disasters, for the country was ill prepared to take the field. The attempt to capture Montreal was a fiasco. American forces suffered resounding defeats at Niagara Falls and Detroit, and lost the garrison at Fort Dearborn, where Chicago now stands. A strong British fleet came up the Chesapeake and assaulted Baltimore and Fort McHenry unsuccessfully. One of the observers during the two-day bombardment of the fort was Francis Scott Key, who was inspired to write the verses of "The Star Spangled Banner."

The British were more successful in their march on Washington from which President Madison and almost everybody else, including a panic-stricken army, had fled across the Potomac into Virginia. Having set fire to the capitol, the presidential mansion, and all government buildings but one, the British returned to their ships and sailed for Jamaica, having suffered very few losses. Built as a red brick structure, the walls of the presidential mansion were so scarred by the fire that it was decided to paint the exterior white, and the mansion soon became known as the White House, with Dolly Madison being the first to renovate the inside.

The War of 1812 aroused sharp criticism on national policies, many sneering at it as "Mr. Madison's War." There were class conflicts about the issue, as well as alarming sectional divisions. In general, political leaders in the South and West were "war hawks," calling for a mass assault on British power. Opposed to them were those speaking for the commercial, financial, and shipping interests of the middle and northeastern states which depended on their trade with Britain for profits.

The Federalists of New England went so far in opposition that they called a convention to meet in secret at Hartford, Connecticut, late in 1814. In its secret sessions, the convention adopted resolutions calling for immediate cessation of the war and the negating of certain federal measures. The New England Federalists went even beyond nullification and indulged in some talk about secession from the Union. Widely denounced for "conspiracy, sedition, and treason," the secret Hartford Convention brought about the collapse of the Federalist party, which soon disintegrated, some remnants of it being picked up later by the Whig party.

Retiring from the White House after his second term in office, Madison was succeeded by his secretary of state, James Monroe, the fourth of the "Virginia dynasty." Madison retired to a substantial manor house, Montpelier, seat of a large plantation he owned in Orange County, Virginia. After retiring to Montpelier, except for a few brief excursions into politics, Madison led a private life. Very studious all his years, he happily spent most of his time reading and editing his papers, particularly the voluminous notes he had taken on the secret proceedings and debates in the Philadelphia Constitutional Convention of 1787.

Fearing that publication of his notes on the secret debates and casual remarks made in that convention might reflect unfavorably on the opinions and reputations of some surviving members of the convention, Madison stipulated that his notes were not to be published until four years after his death, which occurred at the age of eighty-five, early in the summer of 1836.

So it came about that it was not until the 1840s that the American people learned in any illuminating detail of what had gone on at the Philadelphia convention which, after much conflict and with many qualms, had hammered out the Federalist constitution under which the country had been living for more than half a century.

JOHN JAY

John Jay (1745-1829), of Huguenot descent, was born in New York City, attended King's (later Columbia) College, went on to study law, and was admitted to the New York Bar in 1766 at the age of twenty-one, soon establishing his own private practice.

During the tumultuous period leading up to the American Revolution, Jay was a moderate, speaking out against British policies, but certainly without subscribing to the radical democratic-republican views of the Liberty Boys, most of whom he regarded as "lower class," as they were. By birth, training, experience, and personal choice, Jay was always a patrician, sharing Hamilton's views that a propertied elite should hold power.

As a member of the New York delegation to the historic First Continental Congress in 1774, Jay drafted an "Address to the People of Great Britain," which Jefferson, without knowing its authorship, declared to be a "production certainly of the finest pen in America."

Though a reconciliationist, hoping to the last to patch up the differences between the rebellious American colonies and the mother country, Jay served in the Second Continental Congress and in the historic session of 1776 that adopted the Declaration of Independence, which he signed.

Jay drafted the new state constitution for New York, and was later named as minister to Spain. While in Madrid, he was sent to France as one of the three American commissioners who in 1783 negotiated the Treaty of Paris which ended the Revolutionary War and formally recognized American independence. Returning home, Jay was chosen by the Continental Congress to be in charge of foreign affairs, and was in serious difficulties almost immediately.

In 1785, Spain sent Don Diego de Gardoqui to this country as its ambassador extraordinary. Count Gardoqui arrived bringing some tempting offers that might, hopefully, open the way for a mutually profitable trade treaty.

Americans in the South and West, particularly in the states of Virginia and North Carolina which held territories extending westward from the Atlantic to the Mississippi River (territories later to become the states of Kentucky and Tennessee), were vitally concerned about navigation rights on the Mississippi. In the Treaty of Paris of 1763, France had ceded to Spain all of her claims west of the Mississippi, all of the vast and ill-defined expanse known as Louisiana. For most of its length, the river was the boundary between the American and Spanish territories, except that Spain held both banks of the river for several hundred miles above its mouth on the Gulf of Mexico. From New Orleans, a busy and thriving river and ocean port, the Spanish controlled all shipping coming into and passing out of the river. As usual in such cases, Spain made the most of her opportunities, favoring Spanish commerce by imposing restrictions, levies, and tolls on foreign shipping.

This pained many Americans, especially those in the West and South, who wished free and unrestrained shipping down the Mississippi into the Gulf of Mexico. If this right were not obtained, it would impede development of western lands. It would be much cheaper and easier to float heavy agricultural and forest products down the river and out into the Gulf than to cart them laboriously eastward over the mountains.

Madrid had ordered Gardoqui not to yield an inch on Spain's rights along the lower Mississippi. In authorizing Jay to negotiate with Gardoqui, the Continental Congress had strictly instructed him that he was "particularly to stipulate the right of the United States to free navigation of the Mississippi." It is not surprising, therefore, that after more than a year of secret negotiations, no agreement was reached.

Then came a turn that caused widespread alarm and threatened to tear the Union apart. To break the deadlock in negotiations, Secretary Jay recommended to the Continental Congress that his instructions be changed. In a secret session, by a close vote after a bitter debate, the Congress decided that Jay must stop pressing the Mississippi issue, and in return ask for certain trade concessions from Spain.

The motion to change Jay's instructions had the support of seven states, all of the North and East: Massachusetts, Rhode Island, Connecticut, New Hampshire, New York, Pennsylvania, and New Jersey, all of them interested in promoting Atlantic seaboard trade, and having little or no concern about navigation rights on the Mississippi, which, to them, seemed far away and inconsequential. Jay was to agree to a treaty which would close the Mississippi River to navigation for 30 years, in exchange for commercial concessions in the Spanish Caribbean.

Negotiations with Gardoqui were resumed, again in secret, but proved fruitless. The closing of the Mississippi was obviously impossible, since it was apparent that such a treaty would not be ratified by the requisite nine states. The states of the West and South would naturally oppose it. In the summer of 1786, when serving his last term as governor of Virginia, Patrick Henry received a very long letter from his young friend James Monroe, who would succeed Madison as fifth president of the United States. Sitting with the Continental Congress then meeting in New York, detailing the "intrigue" by which Jay had got his instructions changed, Monroe exploded:

> This is one of the most extraordinary transactions I have ever known, a minister negotiating expressly for defeating the object of his instructions, and by a long train of intrigue and management seducing the representatives of the states to concur in it.

In his letter to Patrick Henry, Monroe added even more alarming information. Some influential people of the Northeast were openly talking about the "subject of a dismemberment of the states east of the Hudson from the Union, and the erection of them into a separate government, . . . that the measure is talked about in Massachusetts familiarly, and is supposed to have been originated there. . . ."

Moves to dismember the Union should be blocked, Monroe added, "yet I do consider it as necessary on our part to contemplate it as an event that may happen. . . . It should be so managed (if it takes place) either that it should be formed into three divisions or, if into two, that Pennsylvania, if not Jersey, should be included in ours."

With Patrick Henry taking the lead, the Virginia legislature passed a number of very strong resolutions opposing any attempt "to barter or surrender the rights of the United States to the free and common use of the river Mississippi," that any such attempt would provoke the just resentment "of our western brethren whose essential rights and interests would be thereby sacrificed and sold," that the sacrifice of the rights of certain parts of the Union (the South and West) to the "supposed or real interests" of another part (the North and East) would be "a flagrant violation of justice, a direct contravention of the end for which the federal government was instituted." The fruitless Jay-Gardoqui negotiations were very important to the constitutional convention when the southern states insisted upon a two-thirds majority vote for ratification of treaties. The severely criticized negotiations also became heavily involved in the debate over the role of the senate under the proposed constitution, particularly as it concerned the senate approval of treaties.

In spite of his part in the Gardoqui fiasco, Jay remained in charge of the nation's foreign relations until 1789 when President-elect Washington, recognizing his zealous and influential activities in the Federalist cause, asked Jay which post he wished to occupy in the new administration. Chief justice of the United States, Jay replied, and he was thereupon appointed by and with the consent and advice of the Senate.

In 1792, he resigned to run unsuccessfully for the governorship of New York. Two years later, in 1794, Jay was given another diplomatic assignment, being named by President Washington as special envoy to Great Britain, with whom relations were very strained. In the treaty that resulted, the British complained that they had been "perfectly duped" by Jay. On this side of the Atlantic, Americans, particularly Jeffersonians, sneered at what they called "Jay's treaty" and denounced it as a "give-away." Whatever its defects, which were many, the treaty postponed war with Britain for almost two decades.

Running again for the governorship of New York, this time successfully, Jay served two terms. In 1801, when offered reappointment as chief justice of the United States, he declined and retired to the mansion he had built on his large country estate at Bedford, in Westchester County, New York, dying there in 1829 at the age of eighty-four.

THE FEDERALIST AND ITS BACKGROUND

After the Declaration of Independence in 1776 the states were virtually self-governing. The Articles of Confederation were not effective until ratified by all states, and ratification was not final until 1781. Put together in a hurry at a time of acute crisis, the Articles of Confederation left much to be desired. After suffering the tyranny of King George III and his ministers, the central government was purposely left weak. National power, such as it was, resided in an elected Continental Congress, which met at least once a year. In the Congress each state, whether large or small, had an equal vote (one vote). Each state could send no more than seven nor less than two representatives to Congress, but the delegation voted as a unit after a caucus of its members to determine the views of the majority.

In many areas of legislation, Congress was not empowered to make laws for the country as a whole. It could only recommend that the states take action along the lines suggested. This led to difficulties and confusion. On appropriation bills, for example, Congress would decide that a certain sum of money should be spent for a specific national purpose. But it had no way of raising money directly. All it could do was to call on the states to make their apportioned contributions for the purpose. State legislatures held the purse strings and often were very slow in responding, if they did at all, to what might be called solicitations.

Early in 1781, when the Revolutionary War was still far from being won, Congress asked the states for $8,000,000 to meet emergency national needs. At the end of three years, less than $1,500,000 of this assessment had been paid. On occasion, as New Jersey did in 1786, a state flatly refused to pay anything toward carrying out a Congressional decision of which it disapproved.

As a consequence, in want of ready money, the central government was often delinquent in paying its debts and obligations. This hurt American credit and prestige everywhere. It seemed to a growing number on both sides of the Atlantic that a young nation unable to pay its bills on the due date could not long endure. Many shared Patrick Henry's view that ruin was inevitable unless the national government were given "compulsory process" under which it could collect revenues owed it by delinquent states.

Commercial relations, both domestic and foreign, presented another problem. To protect the economic interests of their citizens, states erected higher and higher tariff barriers against one another. In Connecticut, only hats made in that state could be sold. New York levied duties on firewood brought in from Connecticut, and on vegetables and other farm produce shipped into New York City from New Jersey. Other states imposed similar levies on imports of anything produced outside their boundaries.

Problems on foreign commerce were even more complicated. The nation had great need of negotiating advantageous commercial treaties with the European powers: Britain, France, Spain, Holland, and others. Congress had the right to negotiate such treaties, at least in theory; practically, that right was useless.

As European governments asked, what was the point of negotiating a commercial treaty with the central government when the individual states could exercise their right to tax and regulate foreign commerce as they pleased?

South Carolina, for example, levied a general import duty of 2.5 percent on all foreign goods, with a much higher levy on certain specified articles. Massachusetts prohibited the export of goods on British ships, and doubled the tonnage duty on any goods imported on non-American ships. Similar discriminatory laws in regard to duties, port fees, and other charges were in force in New York, Pennsylvania, Rhode Island, New Hampshire, Maryland, and North Carolina.

To remedy these and other disabilities, a call was sent out to the thirteen states asking them to send delegations to a convention that would consider what revisions should be made in the Articles of Confederation. The convention was to meet in Annapolis, Maryland, but delegates from only five states showed up: Virginia, Delaware, Pennsylvania, New Jersey, and New York. Recognizing that nothing could be done under the circumstances, the delegates—a mere dozen being present—chose Alexander Hamilton to draft an address calling on the states to send delegates to a new convention to be held in Philadelphia on the second Monday in May, 1787.

After five months delay, the Continental Congress cautiously endorsed this plan, saying that it might be "expedient" to hold a constitutional convention "for the sole and express purpose of revising the Articles of Confederation and reporting to Congress and the several legislatures such alterations and provisions therein." In view of developments later, it should be particularly noted here that the convention was called for the "sole and express purpose" of revising the Articles of Confederation, not scrapping them completely, a point that was made much of by the large number of those vigorously opposed to the immediate ratification of the document that finally emanated from Philadelphia.

About three weeks behind schedule, the Philadelphia convention finally got down to work on May 25, 1787. Only seven states were represented, a bare majority, but enough to constitute a quorum. Delegations from five more states soon arrived. Rhode Island boycotted the convention, distrusting the whole project.

For the most part, the delegates were rather young men. Most of them were relatively unknown. The average age of members was forty-four. Out of this younger group came some of the most active and influential leaders in the convention: Alexander Hamilton, age thirty-two; James Madison, thirty-six; Gouverneur Morris of New York, thirty-five; and Charles Pinckney of South Carolina, forty-one.

Some stalwarts of the Revolution were present: Gen. George Washington, age fifty-five; Benjamin Franklin, in his eighties and the oldest member of the convention; George Mason and George Wythe of Virginia; Robert Morris of Pennsylvania, who had been the Confederation's superintendent of finance, becoming known as the "Financier of the Revolution"; Roger Sherman of Connecticut, very democratic in his views, an influential member of the First Continental Congress and a signer of the Declaration of Independence.

Others were absent for various reasons: Sam Adams and John Hancock of Massachusetts; John Adams because he was in London as our ambassador there; Jefferson, our ambassador in Paris; and John Jay, Secretary of Foreign Affairs, busy negotiating with the Spanish about navigation rights on the Mississippi and other troublesome matters. Patrick Henry had been chosen as a member of the Virginia delegation but, for reasons of his own to be discussed later, had declined to serve, as had his old friend and ally, Richard Henry Lee. Lee had submitted to the Continental Congress on June 7, 1776, Virginia's historic resolution, later adopted:

> That these United Colonies are, and of right ought to be free and independent States, that they are absolved from all allegiance to the British Crown....
> That a plan of confederation be prepared and transmitted to the respective Colonies for their consideration and approbation.

When the delegates at Philadelphia got down to business, Washington was elected unanimously to be president of the convention and, though not a parliamentarian, presided very well, with skill and tact. He was impartial in his rulings from the chair, and remained imperturbable even during the angriest clashes of opinion on points of order or procedures of debate. Everybody trusted the cool judgment of "old Stone Face," as some called him without any want of affection or respect.

The convention, having chosen officers and organized itself, decided to sit behind closed doors. All of its proceedings were to be kept secret. Nothing was to be said publicly about what went on without the express approval of the convention. The secrecy rule was well kept.

Jefferson, in Paris, was being kept informed of what was going on in frequent private letters from his young friend Madison. On learning of the secrecy rule, Jefferson pronounced it "abominable." The people had a right to know what was being done in their name on matters of vital concern to all.

Replying to Jefferson, Madison made a good point, saying that secrecy was wise at a time when men were groping and feeling their way toward solutions of many complex problems, trying to reconcile sharply conflicting class and sectional interests. There would be much more freedom of discussion, Madison argued, if the delegates could exchange ideas informally and discuss them "off the record." They would not be committed to a public position from which they might later wish to retire if they changed their minds.

The convention in its first major action decided to go beyond its instructions and authority. It would not devote thought, time, and energy to amending the Articles of Confederation. Rather, it would frame a whole new constitution on quite another foundation, having come to the conclusion "that a national government ought to be established consisting of a supreme Legislature, Judiciary, and Executive."

For that purpose, Virginia submitted a new constitutional plan, drafted largely by Madison and reflecting the views of the larger states. It provided for a president with stronger powers, a supreme court and lesser United States courts, and a legislature of two chambers. In both chambers, state representation should be based on (white) population, and the lower house would be elected by the upper house.

New Jersey objected to this, speaking the view of the smaller states. These insisted that there be but one chamber of the national legislature with equal voice for each state, whatever its population and size, as it had been in the single-chamber Congress under the Articles of Confederation. Connecticut offered a compromise on representation and other matters.

In a remarkably short time, less than four months, the Philadelphia convention managed to put together a proposed new constitution which has proved, by the test of time, to be fundamentally sound though arrived at by any number of compromises, accommodations, and evasions — on the question of slavery, for example, which led to bloody conflict in the Civil War.

Having finished its work, the convention sent its document to the Continental Congress, which accepted it and ordered that copies be sent to the proper state authorities. The latter were to call special conventions to ratify or reject the plan. When and if nine states ratified, the new constitution was to go into effect immediately.

Returning from the Philadelphia convention to Mount Vernon, Washington sent copies of the plan to many of his old and influential friends. One of the first went to Patrick Henry. In a brief but friendly note, Washington remarked to Henry that he was sending the plan without making any "particular observations" about particular points. Washington wrote:

> Your own judgment will at once discover the good and the exceptional parts of it....
> I wish the constitution which is offered had been more perfect; but I sincerely believe it is the best that could be obtained at this time. And as a constitutional door is opened for amendments hereafter, the adoption of it under the present circumstances of the Union is in my opinion desirable.

Patrick Henry, also in a friendly tone, wrote back to say that he could not bring his "mind to accord with the proposed Constitution. The concern I feel on this account is really greater than I am able to express."

Benjamin Franklin, a member of the Philadelphia convention, also had his reservations, taking a very ambiguous and ambivalent attitude: "I agree to this Constitution with all its faults, if they are such, . . . because I expect no better, and because I am not sure that is not the best."

Writing from Paris, Jefferson asked why the Philadelphia convention had assumed the authority—which it did not have—to scrap the Confederation and set out on the uncharted course of writing a whole new constitution for the struggling infant republic. As much good could have been done, he said, if three or four provisions had been added to the Articles of Confederation, "the good old and venerable fabric which should have been preserved, even as a religious relic."

And why the great hurry on the part of some in pushing for immediate ratification, asked Jefferson. The country was at peace and getting along reasonably well; there was no sudden emergency. If it were thought desirable to make a massive shift in the nation's foundations on which to build a whole new framework of government, why not spend a little time in examining the design of the framework, considering alternatives, exploring all possibilities? After this question had been explored and thoroughly discussed throughout the country, why not hold another constitutional convention to review and improve the work done in Philadelphia?

No one held a lower opinion of the proposed constitution than Alexander Hamilton. As a delegate from New York, he had been very active in the Philadelphia convention at first, but his interest soon subsided. Few were interested in his ideas, which were very anti-democratic and, fundamentally, even anti-republican. His notion of the best system of government was that of the British as practiced under king, ministers, and Parliament. The American colonies had successfully revolted against the perversions of this system under George III and his ministers.

For the new American constitution, Hamilton had some very definite ideas: he wanted a very strong executive, an elected president, who was to serve for life, practically as a monarch; this officer would have an absolute veto on any measures passed by the national legislature. He would also have the power to appoint all state governors who would have an absolute veto on all state legislation.

There should be two houses in the national legislature. Members in the upper house (the senate) should be chosen on a property basis, to serve for life. In a bow to "the people," whom he always thoroughly distrusted and disliked ("The people," he once said, "is a great beast") Hamilton conceded the need of a lower house elected by popular vote, but with the vote restricted as narrowly as possible. In his desire for an all-powerful central government, Hamilton would have liked to abolish completely the jurisdictions of the states, reducing them to the status of counties in England. But he did not push this idea, realizing that it was not only impractical but impossible.

Of the new constitution proposed by the Philadelphia convention, Hamilton said: "No man's ideas are more remote from the plan than my own are known to be," and forthwith threw himself into the forefront of those advocating immediate adoption of the proposed plan. He would take what he could get. Anything was better than the Articles of Confederation. "Is it possible," he asked, "to deliberate between anarchy and confusion on one side, and the chance of good to be expected on the other?"

It was Hamilton, as noted before, who conceived the idea of writing a series of newspaper articles arguing for immediate ratification of the plan proposed. He had no difficulty in persuading Madison and Jay to collaborate, but Hamilton did most of the writing, contributing two-thirds of the articles.

The trio worked fast. The first of the long series appeared in the New York City *Independent Journal* late in October, 1787, little more than a month after the Philadelphia convention adjourned. It was Hamilton who arranged to have the articles collected and quickly published in book form as *The Federalist,* in two volumes. The first volume, containing approximately half the articles, was rushed through the press and appeared in March, 1788. The second volume, containing the remainder of the 85 articles, appeared in May.

The Federalist could well have stood some good editing and pruning: it is often repetitious; main themes could have been brought together and better organized. But the authors obviously decided (the decision was probably Hamilton's alone) that there was no time for editing. The book had to be put out and given the widest possible circulation with all speed if it was to have any influence in shaping public opinion as the "Great Debate" on ratification was about to begin.

Consequently, the short newspaper articles were put into the book as originally published. Each short article was numbered as a chapter, with the result that there were 85 chapters of varying lengths — a formidable number. Many a chapter was merely a continuation of an argument begun in the immediately preceding chapters. Such chapters might well have been reworked, revised, and brought together in a single chapter or section. But, as just remarked, "Publius" decided there was no time for that. Speed of publication was the prime essential.

Whatever its faults, *The Federalist* was a masterpiece of its kind. It was closely and cogently reasoned. It met the main issues head-on, with no evasion. It did not deal in invective and personalities, contrary to the fashion of the day; the argument, almost always, was kept on a high, cool level. The writing was strong and good, though it had nothing of the dazzling sparkle of Tom Paine's *Common Sense* (1776) that, almost overnight, fired Americans to strike for independence, a subject which up to that time, as John Adams wrote, had been a "Hobgoblin of so frightful a Mien that it would throw a delicate Person into Fits to look it in the Face."

The impact of *The Federalist* on ratification cannot be measured. Most scholars agree that it was not much. Its arguments were too literate, too sophisticated, and too high-flown to make an impression on the many citizens debating the issue in state legislatures, city councils, town meetings, corner groceries, taverns, or among neighbors gathered around a warm kitchen stove in some remote farmhouse.

But *The Federalist* had a lasting influence. It has become a classic commentary not only on American constitutional law, but on government principles generally, being "equally admirable in the depth of its wisdom, the comprehensiveness of its views, the sagacity of its reflections, and the fearlessness, patriotism, candor, simplicity, and eloquence with which its truths are uttered and recommended." This quotation comes from a Federalist. On a basis of different bias, the great American historian, Charles A. Beard, thought *The Federalist* to be the "finest study in the economic interpretation of politics which exists in any language."

When it appeared, *The Federalist* was not alone in the field. There were many other pamphlets and other publications supporting the Federalist cause. There were quite as many publications supporting anti-Federalist views. Perhaps the most representative and influential of these appeared in *Letters of the Federal Farmer*, written by Richard Henry Lee, a venerable patriot, who had offered the resolution that led to the Declaration of Independence.

Lee objected to the proposed constitution on the ground that, in principle, it was not federalist at all, but "calculated ultimately to make the states one consolidated government." It would erase all state rights, and it said nothing about civil rights: the rights of individual citizens to freedom of speech, freedom of assembly, and such things. Lee's views were shared by other patriots of 1776: Patrick Henry, George Mason, Sam Adams, Thomas Jefferson, among many more. Other anti-Federalist papers and pronouncements, some rather violent in tone, poured from the presses. It was a tense time, with debate raging everywhere.

Such was the stage, rather crowded and noisy, on which *The Federalist* appeared, eager for response from a large miscellaneous audience, north and south, east and west.

SUMMARIES AND COMMENTARIES

The Federalist papers divide logically into a number of sections, with each having a central theme developed in a succession of short chapters.

Consequently, the material will be dealt with in sections. Chapter breaks are indicated for easier reference.

SECTION I, CHAPTERS 1-8
GENERAL INTRODUCTION

The eight chapters in this section laid down the historical groundwork for the arguments on specific constitutional points and political theories to be discussed in detail later.

SUMMARIES

Chapter 1 (Alexander Hamilton)

The opening statement was bold and rather bald, characteristically Hamiltonian in style. The American people, "after an unequivocal experience of the inefficacy of the subsisting Federal Government," were now being called on to consider the adoption of an entirely new United States constitution, a subject of paramount importance. It involved "nothing less than the existence of the UNION . . . the fate of an empire, in many respects, the most interesting in the world." A wrong decision here would "deserve to be considered as the general misfortune of mankind."

Anticipating sharp criticism of the proposed constitution, and active opposition to it, Hamilton grouped dissidents into several categories. There were those constitutionally opposed to any change, no matter what. There were those who feared that a change might cost them their jobs. There were those who liked to fish in troubled waters.

The largest body consisted of men of "upright intentions" whose opposition arose "from sources, blameless at least, if not respectable, the honest errors of minds led astray by preconceived jealousies and fears." This group was "so numerous indeed and so powerful" that it might give a "false bias to the judgment" that would be fatal, leading to a "torrent of angry and malignant passions" aroused by the loudness of their voices and the bitterness of their invective. The debate on both sides should be conducted with moderation, for "nothing could be more ill judged than that intolerant spirit, which has, at all times, characterised political parties."

Hamilton then clearly outlined what was going to be discussed in succeeding essays, particularly the "utility of Union."

Chapter 2 (John Jay)

Picking up the argument, Jay observed, rather fatuously, that government was indispensable, and that it was "equally undeniable, that whenever and however it is instituted, the people must cede to it some of their natural rights in order to vest it with requisite powers."

The central question was this: whether it would be better for Americans to "be one nation, under one federal Government," or "divide themselves into separate confederacies." Some "politicians," as Jay stigmatized the opposition, were saying that instead of looking for safety and happiness in union, it should be sought in a division of the states into distinct confederacies or sovereignties.

Adducing "natural" as well as divine reasons why people should rally to the Federalist cause, Jay observed that America was not composed of detached and distant territories. It was a "connected, fertile, wide spreading country," and "Providence has in a particular manner blessed it with a variety of soils and productions, and watered it with innumerable streams, for the delight and accommodation of its inhabitants."

Providence had also been pleased to give this connected country to one united people, "a people descended from the same ancestors, speaking the same language, professing the same religion, attached to the same principles of government, very similar in their manners and customs. . . . This country and this people seem to have been made for each other, and it appears as if it was the design of Providence, that an inheritance so proper and convenient . . . should never be split into a number of unsocial, jealous and alien sovereignties."

A strong sense of union had pervaded Americans from the day of the Declaration of Independence. In a time of crisis they had set up a central government without having time for "calm and mature enquiries and reflections." It was no wonder then that government (under the Articles of Confederation), "instituted in times so inauspicious, should on experiment be found greatly deficient and inadequate."

Therefore, "intelligent people . . . attached [more] to union, than enamored of liberty," had decided that these ends could be secured only "in a national Government more wisely framed," and "as with one voice, convened the late Convention at Philadelphia."

Chapter 3 (Jay)

All wise and free people directed their attention to "providing for their *safety.*" Was cause of war as "likely to be given by *United America,* as by *disunited* America?"

Noting that some American states bordered on British and Spanish territories, Jay remarked that the borderers, "under the impulse of sudden irritation, and a quick sense of apparent interest or injury," were the most likely to excite war with those nations. In such conflicts, a national government, with its "wisdom and prudence," could effectually diminish the passions of the parties concerned and bring about a peaceful accommodation.

Chapter 4 (Jay)

There were other possible causes of war, Jay went on: "With France and with Britain we are rivals in the fisheries; . . . With them and most other European nations, we are rivals in navigation and the carrying trade; . . . In the trade to China and India, we interfere with more than one nation, in as much as it enables us to partake in advantages which they had in a manner monopolized."

Americans should "consider Union and a good national Government as necessary to put and keep them in *such a situation* as instead of *inviting* war, will tend to repress and discourage it."

If foreign nations "see that our national Government is efficient and well administered . . . they will be much more disposed to cultivate our friendship, than provoke our resentment."

Chapter 5 (Jay)

This essay opened with quotations from a letter by Queen Anne in 1706 when the union of the kingdoms of England and Scotland was under consideration. In her letter to the Scotch Parliament the Queen stressed that if the two kingdoms were "joined in affection and free from all apprehensions of different interest," they could successfully resist any invasion.

As the history of Great Britain was well known to Americans, said Jay, it offered "many useful lessons." Though it would have seemed common sense that the island of Britain should have been one nation, yet the inhabitants were for ages divided into three and "almost constantly embroiled in quarrels and wars with one another."

What if America should be divided into three or four confederacies? How long would these "remain exactly on an equal footing in point of strength?" How long would they remain on friendly terms with one another? Not long. One of the confederacies would soon exceed the others, arousing in them feelings of envy and fear.

As each of the confederacies would be a separate nation, how could they effectively combine their forces against a foreign enemy?

Indeed, could they have a common foreign enemy? The confederacies, each of them, would have their own treaties with foreign governments with regard to the regulation of commerce, etc. "Hence it might and probably would happen that the foreign nation with whom the *Southern* confederacy might be at war, would be the one, with whom the *Northern* confederacy would be the most desirous of preserving peace and friendship." That way lay chaos.

Chapter 6 (Hamilton)

Turning from foreign dangers to a disunited America, this essay took up dangers of a "still more alarming kind, those [that would] in all probability flow from dissentions between the States themselves, and from domestic factions and convulsions."

In spite of all historical experience to the contrary, there were still some "visionary or designing men" (Anti-Federalists) who argued that the American states, even though disunited, would live at peace with one another. They contended that the "genius of republics . . . is pacific; the spirit of commerce has a tendency to soften the manners of men and to extinguish those inflammable humours which have so often kindled into wars." Was this the fact? asked Hamilton, and answered No!

Have republics in practice been less addicted to war than monarchies? Are not the former administered by *men* as well as the latter? . . . Are not popular assemblies frequently subject to the impulses of rage, resentment, jealousy, avarice, and of other irregular and violent propensities? . . .

Has commerce hitherto done any thing more than change the objects of war? Is not the love of wealth as domineering and enterprising a passion as that of power or glory? . . . Has not the spirit of commerce in many instances administered new incentives to the appetite both for the one and the other?

Rome, Carthage, Venice, and Holland were cited to buttress the point that these republics had not been any less warlike than the monarchies of their day. In Britain, for example, commerce had been for ages the predominant pursuit, with the result that few nations "have been more frequently engaged in war;" and such wars had, "in numerous instances proceeded from the people. There have been, if I may so express it, almost as many popular as royal wars."

Away with the reveries that were seducing Americans to believe that, if divided, the several confederacies could peacefully coexist! Hamilton concluded by quoting from an "intelligent writer," l'Abbé de Mably, who in his *Principes des Négociations* laid it down as an unchallenged political axiom that "vicinity, or nearness of situation," makes nations "natural enemies."

Chapter 7 (Hamilton)

Other dangers would face a dismembered America. Territorial disputes, for one thing. Such disputes had always been "one of the most fertile sources of hostility among nations" and existed in the United States along its westward-moving frontier. There had been, and still were, "discordant and undecided claims" by various states to this ill-defined virgin territory. If the union were dissolved, this disputed territory would offer "an ample theatre for hostile pretensions, without any umpire or common judge to interpose between the contending parties."

Also, there would be trade rivalries. States less favorably situated would seek to overcome their disadvantages by moving to share the advantages of more fortunate neighbors. Each state, or separate confederacy, would set up a commercial policy peculiar to itself. The imposition of trade regulations, and efforts to enforce them, would lead to outrages, reprisals, and wars.

Another highly important matter was payment of the Union's public debt. That debt had to be paid if the nation was to maintain its credit at home and abroad. How to pay it would be a further cause of collision between separate states or confederacies.

How would the debt burden be apportioned? The question would arouse ill-humor and animosity. Some states would consider themselves too highly taxed and seek to lessen their burden. Other states would resist this because it would increase their taxes. Here Hamilton added a gem of social and political realism:

> There is perhaps nothing more likely to disturb the tranquility of nations, than their being bound to mutual contributions for any common object, which does not yield an equal and coincident benefit. For it is an observation as true, as it is trite, that there is nothing men differ so readily about as the payment of money.

Chapter 8 (Hamilton)

If accepted as an "established truth" that war between separate parts was probable if the Union were dismembered, such wars between the states would occasion much greater distress than in countries that maintained regular standing armies. Such armies, though dangerous to liberty and economy, had the advantage of rendering sudden conquest impractical and of preventing that rapid desolation which once marked the course of war. The art of fortification had contributed to the same end. Because of their mistrust, the states would delay in setting up regular military establishments. In want of fortifications, the frontiers of one state would be open to another. The populous states, with little difficulty, would overrun their less populous neighbors.

But this condition would not long prevail. Wars and the constant threat of war always "compel nations the most attached to liberty, to resort for repose and security, to institutions, which have a tendency to destroy their civil and political rights. To be more safe they, at length, become willing to run the risk of being less free. The institutions alluded to are STANDING ARMIES, and the correspondent appendages of military establishments." Circumstances would compel the several confederacies at the same time to strengthen the executive arm of government, which would give their constitutions "a progressive direction towards monarchy. It is of the nature of war to increase the executive at the expense of the legislative authority."

In countries requiring standing armies, the continual need for military services "enhances the importance of the soldier, and proportionably degrades the condition of the citizen. The military state becomes elevated above the civil. . . . and by degrees the people are brought to consider the soldiery not only as their protectors, but as their supervisors."

Great Britain was an example of a country that, being insular and protected by a strong navy, had found no need to maintain a large standing army within the kingdom. To this, in large measure, could be attributed the liberty that Britons had long enjoyed.

If the American union were preserved, it would enjoy something of Britain's "insulated situation." Europe was far away. Her colonies in the New World were too weak to be a menace. Extensive military establishments, therefore, would not be needed for American security, but only if the nation stood united under a strong central government.

COMMENTARIES

Chapter 1

The most interesting thing here is Hamilton's analysis of the groups opposing the proposed constitution. There were those congenitally opposed to any change, no matter what. There were those who feared losing status and their jobs under a new arrangement. There were those who always liked to fish in troubled waters, hoping to come up with something. No one denied any of this.

But Hamilton was on more questionable and highly dubious ground when he characterized the main opposition as a lot of well-intentioned men, "blameless at least, if not respectable," who had been led astray "by preconceived jealousies and fears." This large group of well-intentioned but misguided men included a large number of most highly respected patriots from the days of 1776 and before: Thomas Jefferson, Patrick Henry, Richard Henry Lee, George Mason, Sam Adams, and Governor George Clinton of New York, among others. Having blasted the opposition as ignorant, self-seeking, or wrong-headed, Hamilton urged that the debate be conducted with "moderation." This infuriated Anti-Federalists, who took it to mean, as it was intended, that they should keep quiet while Federalists held the floor. Hamilton's tact often left much to be desired.

Chapter 2

A noticeable change of style and approach occurs here where John Jay picked up from Hamilton. Whereas the latter was direct and aggressive, Jay was evasive and liked to make a flank attack. A suave and polished gentleman, Jay liked to belabor platitudes and elaborate the obvious.

Remarking that government was an "indispensable necessity," which no one was denying, Jay declared that Divine Providence "in a particular manner" had blessed the nation with a broad, fertile, well-watered land and populated it with "one united people," descended from the same ancestors, speaking the same language, professing the same religion, and very similar in their manners and customs. Therefore, they should unite in supporting the proposed constitution as the only means of carrying out the "design of Providence."

This was stretching things a bit far. Americans were *not* all descended from the "same ancestors," meaning English. There were many other strains among them: Dutch, German Rhinelanders (the so-called "Pennsylvania Dutch"), Irish, Scotch-Irish, French, Poles, and blacks.

It was true that, except for a few Jews, the people professed the same religion, Christianity, but the conflicts between the many denominations of that faith were fierce. The Puritan Congregationalists of New England; the high-toned Episcopalians in New York, Virginia, and states to the south; the Pennsylvania Quakers; the Scotch Presbyterians; the Welsh Dissenters, many of whom were Baptists; the Methodists; and the Dutch and German Lutherans were constantly at odds.

Chapter 3

Jay here took up the question of war, which seems to have been a preoccupation with the Federalists. At least, they talked a great deal about it, although admitting that the chances of war were remote.

Still, if war came, it could be more successfully waged by a closely-knit union under the proposed constitution. There would be one supreme military command. All states would be united in purpose and making their fair contributions of men and money. The new order would control the "improper conduct of individual States" which had provoked many Indian wars along the frontier. This last control would do much in promoting "domestic" tranquility.

Jay did not have the foresight to see that, no matter what the constitution was, attacks would continue unabated against the Indians until they were almost exterminated.

Chapter 4

Jay continued on war and observed that Americans were rivals with European powers in the fisheries, in navigation and the carrying trade, in commerce with China, the Spice Islands, and India where European nations had held a virtual monopoly. Jay asked: what if the European powers, singly or in combination, struck at the United States and its expanding economic interests? What would be the best defense? The answer: a strong federal government able to mobilize all its resources immediately for effective use—all of which is so obvious that it would seem scarcely worth elaborating.

Chapter 5

Jay next dealt with dangers that "almost certainly" would arise if the union were split into separate confederacies, each a sovereign nation having its own commercial and other treaties with foreign powers, which would lead to rivalries and conflicts of interest.

Jay made a good point here in saying that "the foreign nation with whom the *Southern* confederacy might be at war, would be the one, with whom the *Northern* confederacy would be the most desirous of preserving peace and friendship." Here Jay anticipated what more or less happened in the War of 1812, when the interests of the West and the South precipitated a war much to the disadvantage of New England.

Chapter 6

Picking up the text here, Hamilton developed the argument that dismemberment of the Union would present another danger of a "still more alarming kind": the danger of "domestic factions and convulsions."

Here Hamilton's fundamental principles of political philosophy came to the fore, though not too openly, being slightly masked. Anything smacking of democracy was an anathema to him; democracy meant tumult and "convulsions." Even republics were suspect in his eyes. They were apt "to waste themselves in ruinous contentions." Had commercial republics, "like ours," been less addicted to war than monarchies?

Taking a shot at "visionary or designing men," meaning the Anti-Federalists, Hamilton denied their view that commerce had "a tendency to soften the manners of men and to extinguish those inflammable humours which have so often kindled into wars." That was not so. Commerce merely increased the appetite for wealth and dominion, as most clearly evidenced in the history of Great Britain, a great commercial nation, which had been "more frequently engaged in war" than almost any other. Americans should put away the "fallacy and extravagance of those idle theories which have amused us with promises of an exemption from the imperfections, weaknesses and evils incident to society in every shape."

Chapter 7

Hamilton then pointed out other dangers that would face a dismembered union: territorial disputes, for one thing. A number of states had claims to parts of a vast tract of unsettled territory along the country's westward-moving frontier. There had already been trouble about this, even armed skirmishes. How could conflicting state claims be settled peaceably without a federal government which could act as "umpire or common judge to interpose between the contending parties"?

There was another matter of paramount importance: how to pay the public debt of the union? All states should contribute to paying off that debt, but how? and in what proportions? What power was to decide that question? Would some states resist, or evade? It was a very difficult problem, Hamilton admitted, for no one liked to lay out money.

Chapter 8

Having demonstrated to his own satisfaction the "established truth" that if the union were dismembered, war between the separate parts was "probable," Hamilton sagely observed that the constant threat of war always compels nations, even those most attached to liberty, to seek security in institutions having a tendency to destroy their civil and political rights — such institutions being "STANDING ARMIES, and the correspondent appendages of military establishments."

Such armies were a standing threat to the liberties of the people, elevating the soldier over the civilian. They tended to strengthen the executive arm of government so that it moved in a "progressive direction towards monarchy . . . at the expense of the legislative authority."

Britons had long enjoyed a large measure of civil liberties, and Hamilton was partly right in attributing this to the fact that Britain, being insular and protected by a strong navy, had not found it necessary to keep a large standing army. Americans enjoyed a somewhat similar "insulated situation." If the union were preserved and had a strong volunteer militia under a national commander-in-chief, the country would have no need of a standing army and extensive military establishments. This would save vast sums of money better spent on more productive things than killing and being killed.

SECTION II, CHAPTERS 9-14
ADVANTAGES OF UNION

This section, consisting of six papers (Chapters 9-14), discusses the advantage of union in general, and not the advantages of a particular form of union as set forth in the proposed constitution.

SUMMARIES

Chapter 9 (Hamilton)

A firm union acts to prevent domestic faction and insurrection. A reading of the histories of the petty republics of Greece and Italy caused such "sensations of horror and disgust at the distractions with which they were continually agitated" that advocates of despotism had drawn arguments not only against all forms of republican government, but against the very principles of civil liberty.

"The science of politics, however, like most other sciences has received great improvement . . . not known at all, or imperfectly known to the ancients," said Hamilton, who went on to quote at length from the great French political philosopher, Montesquieu, whose *Spirit of the Laws* had become a classic.

Extracting from this work what suited his argument, Hamilton cited Montesquieu on the advantages of what the latter called a "Confederate Republic, . . . a kind of assemblage of societies, that constitute a new one, capable of encreasing by means of new associations, till they arrive to such a degree of power as to be able to provide for the security of the united body. A republic of this kind, able to withstand an external force, may support itself without any internal corruption." The American republic, if placed under the proposed constitution, would answer that description.

Chapter 10 (James Madison)

This essay, the first of Madison's contributions to the series, was a rather long development of the theme that a well-constructed union would break and control the violence of faction, a "dangerous vice" in popular governments.

As defined by Madison, a faction was a number of citizens, whether a majority or minority, who were united and activated "by some common impulse of passion, or of interest, adverse to the rights of other citizens, or to the permanent and aggregate interests of the community."

There were two ways of removing the causes of factions, or political parties. The first was to destroy the liberty essential to their existence. This remedy would be worse than the disease. The second was to give everyone the same opinions, passions, and interests. This was impossible. Woven into the fabric of all societies, deeply planted in the very nature of man, were conflicting ideas, interests, and passions. The greatest source of factions had always been the various and unequal distribution of property, said Madison:

> Those who hold, and those who are without property, have ever formed distinct interests in society. Those who are creditors, and those who are debtors, . . . a landed interest, a manufacturing interest, a mercantile interest, a monied interest, with many lesser interests, grow up of necessity in civilized nations, and divide them into different classes, actuated by different sentiments and views. The regulation of these various and interfering interests forms the principal task of modern Legislation.
>
> The inference to which we are brought, is, that the *causes* of faction cannot be removed; and that relief is only to be sought in the means of controlling its *effects*.

Such effects could be better controlled in a large society under a representative form of government than in a small society under a popular form of government. The proposed constitution would check the power of factions by balancing one against the other. Factious leaders might "kindle a flame" in one state, but would be unable to spread a general conflagration throughout the states.

"A rage for paper money, for abolition of debts, for an equal division of property, or for any other improper or wicked project, . . ." was not likely to spread if those professing themselves republicans showed zeal in "supporting the character of Federalists."

Chapter 11 (Hamilton)

Repeating himself somewhat, Hamilton declared that a closer union would greatly benefit American commerce. The growth of the nation's trade and shipping had already led European maritime powers to think of clipping "the wings by which we might soar to a dangerous greatness." Essential to the growth of American economy was the creation of a federal navy of sufficient strength to make its weight felt in the world. Such an armed naval force would enable the country to bargain with great advantage for commercial rights and privileges.

Unrestrained trade among the states, as proposed in the new constitution, would also be a boon. Working closely together, the states could supply one another's differing needs and produce a surplus for export on American ships.

America should "aim at the ascendant." Too long had Europe lorded it over the world, as if the "rest of mankind [were] created for her benefit." Europeans, including some so-called "profound philosophers," had gone to the length of asserting that all animals, including the human species were so "degenerate in America—that even dogs cease to bark after having breathed a while in our atmosphere." It was time that such "arrogant pretensions" be disproved.

"It belongs to us to vindicate the honor of the human race. . . . Let Americans disdain to be the instruments of European greatness!" If the states were closely joined under a federal constitution, they would be able "to dictate the terms of the connection between the old and the new world!"

Chapter 12 (Hamilton)

A new union would increase governmental revenues and facilitate their collection. The development of commerce would make it easier not only to pay taxes, but to collect them. The greater part of national revenues should come from the imposition of customs duties and various excises, which would be "imperceptible . . . taxes on consumption."

In France, said Hamilton, fifteen percent of national revenues came from import duties and domestic excises; in Britain, even more. American revenues from such sources could easily be trebled.

Chapter 13 (Hamilton)

A firm union would bring economy in the operations and costs of government. There would be just "one national civil list" to support. Some men were talking of dividing the country into three confederacies, "one consisting of the four northern, another of the four middle, and a third of the five southern States." Each of these confederacies would be at the expense of supporting a whole elaborate governmental apparatus.

Hamilton then speculated on the difficult problems certain states would face in the event of dismemberment, which he used to point his conclusion that "separation would be not less injurious to the economy than to the tranquillity, commerce, revenue and liberty of every part."

Chapter 14 (Madison)

This chapter is a summary of the main points made in the preceding essays of this section.

COMMENTARIES

Chapter 9

The disquisitions here by Hamilton on the weaknesses of the petty republics in ancient Greece and Italy were not good history, being rather superficial, but made good argument for the large Federalist plan of government he favored. Hamilton was also rather partisan in the passages he chose to quote from Montesquieu's *Spirit of the Laws.*

Chapter 10

Madison's definition of a "faction," or political party, is interesting and most significant in view of the fact that Madison soon ceased to be one of the Federalists who believed in a one-party system, and became Jefferson's most active lieutenant in organizing in opposition the Democratic-Republican Party, which was strongly Anti-Federalist and took power after 1800.

Chapter 11

Hamilton elaborated on his point that a close union would greatly benefit American commerce, particularly if protected by a strong Navy. Europeans with their "arrogant pretensions" that the world belonged to them should be put in their place. Americans would thus "vindicate the honor of the human race" and be able "to dictate the terms" between the Old World and the New.

Chapter 12

What should be noted here is Hamilton's statement that, in raising revenues for national governments, the levying of taxes on property and income had proved to be impractical. Hence, if the proposed constitution were adopted, the new national government would raise a large part of its revenues from customs duties, excise taxes, and similar imposts – or by what Hamilton called the "imperceptible agency of taxes on consumption," or what we now call a sales tax.

Chapter 13

No one could deny Hamilton's argument here that the costs of supporting a national governmental apparatus would be less if the country remained united, instead of being split into two or three sovereign confederacies, each of which would have to have its own governmental apparatus.

Chapter 14

This chapter is a good summary of the main points made by Publius up to this point in the book.

SECTION III, CHAPTERS 15-22
DISADVANTAGES OF EXISTING GOVERNMENT

This section contains eight essays, Chapters 15-22, centered on the theme that the United States could not long survive if the country continued to be governed under the Articles of Confederation, and emphasizing the point that the crisis was imminent and necessitated immediate action against "impending anarchy."

SUMMARIES

Chapter 15 (Hamilton)

The point next in order, wrote the author, is the "insufficiency of the present confederation to the preservation of the Union," an insufficiency that had led the country to the "last stage of humiliation," being both weak at home and flouted abroad.

The chief vice of the Confederation lay "in the principle of LEGISLATION for STATES or GOVERNMENTS, in their CORPORATE or COLLECTIVE CAPACITIES as contradistinguished from the INDIVIDUALS of whom they consist." The consequence was that the resolutions of Congress were not laws, but mere recommendations to the states, which accepted or rejected them as they chose. "The authority of the union," under a "general DISCRETIONARY SUPERINTENDENCE," should be extended "to the persons of the citizens,—the only proper objects of government."

Government implies the power to make laws; laws, if they are to mean anything at all, have to be attended with a "sanction"—that is, a penalty or punishment for disobedience. Under the Confederation, the central government did not have the authority or the power to impose penalties on recalcitrant states, which left it a mere shadow of government, scarcely deserving the name. With what result?

"The measures of the Union have not been executed; and the delinquencies of the States have step by step matured themselves to an extreme; which has at length arrested all the wheels of the national government, and brought them to an awful stand . . . 'till the frail and tottering edifice seems ready to fall upon our heads and to crush us beneath its ruins."

Chapter 16 (Hamilton)

Citing the generally unfortunate experience of confederacies in the ancient world, Hamilton continued his argument by saying that the principle of confederacy was the "parent of anarchy," and an almost certain cause of war. If the union under the Articles of Confederation, not having a large army at its disposal, decided to move against recalcitrant states, such action would bring on war between some states and others —a war in which the "strongest combination would be most likely to prevail, whether it consisted of those who supported, or of those who resisted the general authority."

That would mark the "violent death of the Confederacy," said Hamilton. "Its more natural death is what we now seem to be on the point of experiencing, if the federal system be not speedily renovated in a more substantial form." To be capable of regulating common concerns and preserving general tranquility, a federal government had to extend its agency to the persons of the citizens to be properly constituted. "It must stand in need of no intermediate legislations; but must itself be empowered to employ the arm of the ordinary magistrate to execute its own resolutions. . . . The government of the Union, like that of each State, must be able to address itself immediately to the hopes and fears of individuals."

To the argument that under such a constitution some states might still be recalcitrant, Hamilton replied by drawing a distinction between "mere NON COMPLIANCE and a DIRECT and ACTIVE RESISTANCE." As things stood, state legislatures could decide not to act, or to act evasively, on national measures. Under the proposed new constitution, laws of the national government would go by state legislatures and pass into immediate operation upon the citizens themselves. Thus, state legislatures could not block or circumvent execution of the supreme law of the land. If they attempted to do so, their action would be clearly unconstitutional and void, and their constituents, if "not tainted," would rally to the support of the national government.

If opposition to the national government arose on the part of "refractory or seditious" individuals, that could be overcome by the same means daily used by state governments against that evil. As to those "mortal feuds" that in certain situations spread like a conflagration through a whole nation, or a large part of it, occasioned by "weighty causes of discontent given by the government, or from the contagion of some violent popular paroxysm," such upheavals usually resulted in resolution and dismemberment of empires, and were beyond the ordinary rules of calculation. No form of government can always avoid such great uprisings, or contain them.

"It is in vain to hope to guard against events too mighty for human foresight or precaution," Hamilton concluded, "and it would be idle to object to a government because it could not perform impossibilities."

Chapter 17 (Hamilton)

In answer to the argument that the principle of legislating for individual citizens would tend to make the central government too powerful and tempt it to usurp powers proper to the states in regulating purely local affairs, Hamilton replied that this was most unlikely. Federal councils would not be tempted to get into local affairs because such action would contribute nothing "to the dignity, to the importance, or to the splendour of the national government."

Indeed, the danger was the other way round. Being closer to the people, state governments could more easily encroach upon the national authorities than the latter upon state authorities.

Hamilton cited the ancient feudal systems as an example of the experience of all confederate systems. While admitting that the analogy was not strictly true, Hamilton maintained that the feudal systems "partook of the nature" of confederacies. There was a sovereign, or chieftain, with authority over the whole nation; under him were a number of subordinate vassals, or feudatories, holding vast lands; and under the feudatories, or barons, were numerous inferior vassals and retainers who held their lands at the pleasure of the barons.

"Each principal vassal was a kind of sovereign within his particular demesnes." The result was continual opposition to the sovereign's authority and frequent wars between the great barons themselves, a period known to historians as "the times of feudal anarchy."

There occasionally appeared a superior sovereign who, through personal weight and influence, managed to establish some order and keep the peace. But in general, Hamilton observed, "the power of the barons triumphed over that of the prince; and in many instances his dominion was entirely thrown off, and the great fiefs were erected into independent principalities or states. . . . The separate governments in a confederacy may aptly be compared with the feudal baronies. . . ."

Chapters 18-20 (Madison and Hamilton)

Madison went on with the historical analogies, digging into ancient history to consider the Amphictyonic Council of ancient Greece. Made up of independent Greek city states, all of them republics, the council bore, in Madison's view, "a very instructive analogy to the present confederation of the American States." Rivalries and conflicts of interest among the members of the council led to weaknesses and disorders, and finally to internecine wars that wrecked this early confederacy.

It was succeeded by the Achaean League, another society of Greek republics. The league worked better than the council because the central governing body had more authority. But that authority was not strong enough, with the result that the league fell apart into warring factions. Foreign princes began playing one side against the other. The Romans were invited to come in by one faction, and the Romans never left, soon reducing all of Greece to a dependency, extinguishing the "last hope of ancient liberty."

Madison next took up the problems of what he called the "Germanic Body," noting that the Germanic tribes had approximated themselves into seven distinct nations. Among these were the Franks, who conquered the Gauls and established a kingdom. By the end of the eighth century Charlemagne, as King of France, conquered most of Germany and made it part of his vast empire. Later, when the empire weakened, the principal German vassals, whose fiefs had become hereditary, threw off the imperial yoke and set themselves up as independent sovereigns.

But there remained a Diet, a legislative assembly, an arm of a German confederacy. The Diet had general powers in legislating for the empire, subject to the emperor's veto. From its constitutional structure, one might suppose that the German confederacy would be an exception to the general character of confederacies. Quite the contrary, said Madison. The history of Germany was a history of civil wars and foreign invasions, of oppression of the weak by the strong, and "of general imbecility, confusion and misery."

Anticipating argument, Madison declared that the connection among the Swiss cantons scarcely amounted to a confederacy, though sometimes cited as an instance of the stability of such institutions. The Swiss had no common treasury, no common troops, no common coin, no common judiciary, nor any common mark of sovereignty. The Swiss cantons were held together "by the peculiarity of their topographical position, by their individual weakness and insignificancy, by the fear of powerful neighbors."

Remarking that the United Netherlands was a confederacy of seven equal and sovereign republics, Madison went at considerable length into the constitutional structure of that country. Summing up his findings about the "celebrated Belgic confederacy," Madison asked what had been its general character and answered, at least to his own satisfaction:

> Imbecility in the government; discord among the provinces; foreign influence and indignities; a precarious existence in peace, and peculiar calamities from war.

In concluding this part of the essay series, Madison said he had no apology to make "for having dwelt so long on the contemplation of these federal precedents."

Madison used, to the point of tedium, detailed historical analogies and often dubious and generally simplistic contemplations on what he pronounced to be the universal failure of confederacies.

Chapter 21 (Hamilton)

In this essay, after wandering around a bit on rather soggy ground, the author comes to his main point: the disabilities of the American central government under the Articles of Confederation.

Reiterating what he had said more than once in previous essays, Hamilton emphasized that the chief defect in the existing national government was its "total want of a SANCTION to its laws." It had no power to command obedience, or to punish disobedience. The situation posed not only foreign but domestic dangers. A faction might subvert a state constitution and "trample upon the liberties of the people, while the national government could legally do nothing more than behold [this] . . . with indignation and regret." A case in point was the "tempestuous situation" from which Massachusetts had just emerged. Hamilton was here referring to Shay's Rebellion which occurred late in 1786.

Who can determine what might have been the issue of [Massachusetts] late convulsions, if the mal-contents had been headed by a Caesar or by a Cromwell? Who can predict what effect a despotism established in Massachusetts, would have upon the liberties of New-Hampshire or Rhode-Island; of Connecticut or New-York?

Another fundamental error of the Confederation was the principle of assigning individual states a quota of money to be contributed to the national treasury. First, this did not raise sufficient revenue because many states were delinquent in meeting their quotas. Second, a matter of equity was involved. Neither the value of lands nor the size of population, which had been established as the rule for determining state quotas, was equitable.

There was "no common measure of national wealth; and of course, no general or stationary rule, by which the ability of a State to pay taxes can be determined." The national government should be authorized "to raise its own revenues in its own way [by] imposts, excises and in general all duties upon articles of consumption" which would tend, in time, to level off to the individual's ability to pay. If they did not buy something, they would not be taxed for it.

"Impositions of this kind usually fall under the denomination of indirect taxes," Hamilton concluded, "and must always constitute the chief part of the revenue raised in this country."

Chapter 22 (Hamilton)

Another major defect in the existing national government was its lack of power to regulate commerce, both interstate and foreign. There was no field that more immediately needed "Federal superintendence." The states erected tariff barriers against one another and, in ocean commerce, made their own regulations about foreign trade and shipping.

As to raising armies, the existing government had only the power to make requisitions upon the states for quotas of men. During the Revolution, this had led to great inefficiency and "gave birth to a competition between the States, which created a kind of auction for men."

Those nearest the area of combat, for mere survival, raised more troops; those farther removed, fewer. The whole faulty system resulted in the "slow and scanty levies of men in the most critical emergencies in our affairs — short enlistments at an unparalleled expense — continual fluctuations in the troops, ruinous to their discipline, and subjecting the public safety frequently to the perilous crisis of a disbanded army."

The whole system of quotas and requisitions on states in regard to men and money was, from every view, "a system of imbecility in the union, and of inequality and injustice among the members."

The inequality was shown very glaringly in the fact that all states had an equal voice in making decisions under the Confederation. This principle gave "to Rhode-Island an equal weight in the scale of power with Massachusetts, or Connecticut, or New-York; and to Delaware, an equal voice in the national deliberations with Pennsylvania or Virginia, or North-Carolina." A sixtieth part of the union, "about the proportion of Delaware and Rhode-Island," had several times prevented the Confederation from doing anything at all about important measures. This violated the "fundamental maxim of republican government, which requires that the sense of the majority should prevail."

But the crowning defect of the Confederation was its want of judiciary power. Who was to have the final say in determining what the national law was? There should be "one court paramount to the rest — possessing a general superintendence, and authorized to settle and declare in the last resort, an uniform rule of civil justice."

All told, the Confederation was a "system so radically vicious and unsound, as to admit not of amendment but by an entire change in its leading features and characters." It was "one of the most execrable forms of government . . . ever contrived. . . . The fabric of American Empire ought to rest on the solid basis of THE CONSENT OF THE PEOPLE. The streams of national power ought to flow immediately from that pure original fountain of all legitimate authority."

COMMENTARIES

Chapter 15

Hamilton here again stressed that the "insufficiency" of the American Confederation arose from the fact that there was no general "superintendence," and such superintendence should be extended beyond the confederated state governments to the people themselves in their persons as citizens, "the only proper objects of government."

Under the Articles of Confederation, the central government had no power to make laws and impose "sanctions" for disobedience. The central government made recommendations which the states followed or not, as they pleased. The result was a shambles, with the "frail and tottering" governmental structure ready to collapse on everybody's head.

The situation was not nearly as desperate as Hamilton painted it for the purpose of advancing his own arguments. But it was generally agreed that some constitutional changes (not necessarily those advocated in *The Federalist*) might well improve things.

Chapters 16-20

In these five essays Madison and Hamilton belabor their contention that the principle of confederacy was the "parent of anarchy," as well as the fertile soil for wars both civil and foreign.

Digging into history to buttress their contention with analogies, it was ingenious, to say the least, to assert that the feudal systems during the Dark Ages and Middle Ages in Europe "partook of the nature of confederacies." To compare the thirteen confederated American states with the oppressive and constantly warring feudal baronies was certainly far-fetched, but Hamilton pursued his point that America was rapidly approaching "times of feudal anarchy."

Nor were the analogies from the history of ancient Greece much more germane. The Greek city states — Athens, Sparta, Thebes, and others — had deeper and more serious problems than the exact terms of their confederated cooperation in the Amphictyonic Council and its successor, the Achaean League, both of which failed of their purpose.

The analogies drawn from the history of the "Germanic Body," and from the histories of Switzerland and Holland were even less accurate.

Madison and Hamilton went out of their way to declare that the close cooperation among the Swiss cantons did not constitute a confederacy at all, and that the United Netherlands, a confederation of seven Dutch republics, was an "imbecility in government."

What the authors refrained from remarking was that the Swiss and the Dutch people, whatever their governmental "imbecility," were better off, for the most part, than the people ruled by "strong" governments in the monarchies of Britain, France, Spain, Russia, and the fragmented German and Italian states and principalities.

Chapter 21

Getting back on more familiar ground where his footing was surer, Hamilton summarized his objections to the existing central government under several headings:

First, its "total want of a SANCTION to its laws." It could not command obedience, or punish disobedience.

Second, the principle of assigning to states a quota of money to be paid into the national treasury. States were often in arrears, and on occasion refused to pay anything toward carrying out measures of which they disapproved. The national government should have the power to raise revenue in its own way, preferably, Hamilton suggested, by what were virtually sales taxes in the form of "imposts, excises and in general all duties upon articles of consumption." Hamilton did not note that sales taxes fall harder upon the poor than the rich.

Third, the government's want of power to regulate commerce, whether interstate or foreign.

Fourth, the government's inability to raise troops except by requisitioning quotas of men from the states. The whole system of quotas to raise men and money was an "imbecility in the Union."

Fifth, the fact that under the Confederation each state, large or small, whether quite populous or much less populous, had an equal right (one state, one vote) in the decision-making of the central government created injustice and inequality. It violated the "fundamental maxim of republican government, which requires that the sense of the majority should prevail."

Sixth, the crowning defect of the Confederation was its want of judiciary power. There should be one supreme court, "possessing a general superintendance" and authorized to "declare in the last resort, a uniform rule of civil justice."

The American central government was "one of the most execrable forms of government . . . ever contrived . . . a system so radically vicious and unsound, as to admit not of amendment but by an entire change in its leading features and characters."

The only way to avoid impending disaster was the swiftest possible ratification of the proposed new constitution, argued Hamilton, although, as noted before, he thoroughly disapproved of the Philadelphia document, accepting it only because, along with Washington and others, he thought that it was as good as could be expected under the circumstances.

Chapter 22

In this essay Hamilton made several strong points about the lack of power of the national government under the Confederation.

For one thing, it could not regulate or control either interstate or foreign commerce. The states erected high tariff barriers against one another. (The basic clause in the Articles of Confederation read: "...each State retains its sovereignty, freedom, and independence.") For example, only hats made in Connecticut could be sold in that state, making Danbury "the Hat City," as it is still known. New York levied duties on firewood brought in from Connecticut, and on vegetables from New Jersey.

Patrick Henry, once an eloquent advocate of Free Trade, turned provincial in the 1780s and, as a member of the House of Delegates, proposed that the Virginia legislature prohibit the importation from other states or foreign nations of any beef, pork, butter, cheese, or distilled liquor, and that heavy duties be imposed to discourage the import of coal, iron, and cordage. The Virginia legislature did not go as far as Henry proposed, but considerably increased duties on beef, strong drink, and other items.

Foreign trade presented a different but rather similar problem. To increase its export and import business, the infant republic had great need to negotiate advantageous commercial treaties with European nations. The national government had the right to negotiate such treaties, but the right was largely theoretical. As European diplomats asked, what was the point of negotiating a commercial treaty with the national government so long as the individual states could tax and regulate foreign trade as they pleased?

South Carolina, for instance, levied a general tax of 2.5 percent on foreign imports, with much higher rates for certain specified articles. Massachusetts prohibited the export of American goods on British ships; it doubled the tonnage duties on goods imported on other than American ships. New York, Pennsylvania, Maryland, North Carolina, Rhode Island, and New Hampshire had similar discriminatory laws against foreign shipping and trade.

The greatest of the Confederation's disabilities was the fact that the Continental Congress did not have the authority to raise any revenue directly for the support of the national government in carrying out its various functions. When Congress passed an appropriation bill for a specific purpose, all it could do was to *request* the states to contribute their allotted share of the general assessment. As states did not like to tax their own people for general purposes, it is no wonder that many of them were very slow in paying.

In 1781, before the Revolution had been won, Congress asked the states for $8,000,000 to meet emergency needs. At the end of three years, less than $1,500,000 of this assessment had been paid. A number of states followed the example of New Jersey which, in 1786, refused to pay a penny toward carrying out Congressional decisions they disapproved of.

Consequently, in want of ready money, the national government was often delinquent in meeting its debts and obligations, which hurt American credit and prestige. There was a growing opinion on both sides of the Atlantic that a young nation, apparently unable to pay its domestic and foreign debts when due, could not long endure.

SECTION IV, CHAPTERS 23-29
COMMON DEFENSE

This section, consisting of seven essays, addressed itself to the question of how best to defend the American people against foreign aggression.

SUMMARIES

Chapter 23 (Hamilton)

Essential to common defense was the authority to raise armies, build and equip a navy, direct their operations, and provide for their support. The Confederation recognized this but lacked the requisite means to carry it out. To raise men and money, it had to rely on a "fallacious scheme of quotas and requisitions" from the individual states.

There should be a single national government with authority to act "without limitation" because of the impossibility of foreseeing the nature and extent of national emergencies, or what means might be required to meet them. If the proposed constitution were adopted, there was no reason to fear that the central government would abuse such unlimited authority.

Chapter 24 (Hamilton)

Reverting in a rather long essay to the subject of standing armies in times of peace, Hamilton noted that the constitutions of Pennsylvania and North Carolina contained this provision: "as standing armies in time of peace are dangerous to liberty, *they ought not* to be kept up." The constitutions of Massachusetts, New Hampshire, Maryland, and Delaware contained similar provisions. That was beside the point, argued Hamilton.

Under the proposed constitution, the power of raising military forces would be "lodged in the *legislature,* not in the *executive,*" and that legislature would consist of representatives periodically elected by the people themselves. That should provide adequate control.

"If we mean to be a commercial people or even to be secure on our Atlantic side, we must endeavour as soon as possible to have a navy." A navy would need dockyards and arsenals, and "moderate garrisons" of a standing military force would be necessary to guard these.

Chapter 25 (Hamilton)

A great danger to the country came from the fact that territories of Britain, Spain, and various Indian nations encircled the Union. Some states were more exposed than others. Should such states bear all the weight of measures taken to secure their safety? Or should all states join in defending national security by means "of common councils and of a common treasury"? A standing military force would also be useful in quelling domestic insurrections, such as Massachusetts had recently experienced by Shay's Rebellion.

Chapter 26 (Hamilton)

The idea of limiting legislative authority for providing national defense was, in Hamilton's words, "one of those refinements, which owe their origin to a zeal for liberty more ardent than enlightened."

Taking Britain as an example, Hamilton briefly cited what had happened there before, during, and after the Glorious Revolution of 1688, which dethroned James II for tyranny and abuse of authority. For one thing, the king had in time of peace increased the standing army in the kingdom from 5,000 to 30,000 men. After the revolution, the British Parliament framed a Bill of Rights that contained this article: "That the raising or keeping a standing army within the kingdom in time of peace *unless with the consent of parliament* is against law."

Chapter 27 (Hamilton)

A national government along the lines proposed would have less occasion to use force in obtaining compliance with its laws than in a loose confederation with no strong central power.

Chapter 28 (Hamilton)

Seditions and insurrections now and again occur in all societies and are to the body politic what "tumors and eruptions" are to the human body. If such emergencies arose under the national government, there could be "no remedy but force," with means proportioned to the extent of the "mischief." Individual states through their own militias could themselves handle minor commotions.

Chapter 29 (Hamilton)

National security demanded that the central government have the power to regulate the state militias and command their services in times of invasion or insurrection. Uniformity in the organization and discipline of the militias would greatly increase their proficiency on the field of battle. The states would appoint the officers of their militias and have the authority of training such forces *"according to the discipline prescribed by Congress."* There was no danger to be apprehended to the political rights and civil liberties of the American people by such federal "general superintendence" of the militias.

COMMENTARIES

Chapters 23-29

In these essays, Hamilton wished to substantiate his main lines of argument, which were two: first, that American security depended on a national system of defense under the direction and control of a strong central government; and second, that a well-organized military force would not be a threat to the political liberties and civil rights of the people if, as proposed, all armed forces were placed under the control of the legislature, the Congress, consisting of popularly elected representatives of the people. If such representatives betrayed the people, then the latter would have the right to rise up as they had in their revolution against British rule.

SECTION V, CHAPTERS 30-36
POWERS OF TAXATION

This section of seven chapters analyzes the many problems involved in setting up a just and equitable system of taxation, and in reconciling the conflicting claims of various taxing authorities at all levels of government—federal, state, and local.

SUMMARIES

Chapter 30 (Hamilton)

The national government under the Articles of Confederation lacked the revenues necessary for carrying out its purposes because a faulty fiscal system made it dependent on quotas and requisitions from the thirteen individual states. A national government, properly constituted, should have the power to raise its own revenues by the methods of taxation ordinarily used in every well-ordered "civil government."

Adequate national revenues, as some argued, could not be raised by "external" taxes alone, i.e., by customs duties on foreign imports. The central government should be empowered to levy "internal" taxes also, as necessity required.

Chapter 31 (Hamilton)

Opening this essay with a disquisition on the eternal verities of geometry and other sciences, Hamilton observed that politics was not an exact science because it dealt with the "unruly passions of the human heart," and therefore tended to be rather irrational. Among the more irrational, Hamilton added, were those who opposed the proposed constitution from fear that the national government by its "unlimited" taxing measures might deprive the states of the means of providing for their own needs.

It would be the other way around if this point came into contest, said Hamilton. It was probable that the states, being closer to the people, would encroach more on the revenue-raising plans of the central government than otherwise.

Chapter 32 (Hamilton)

States should retain their "independent and uncontrollable authority to levy taxes for their own purposes, with the exception of laying customs duties on foreign imports and exports, or tariffs on any articles in interstate commerce. There was to be absolutely free trade among the states, which would stimulate the national economy.

Chapter 33 (Hamilton)

Opponents of ratification were raising objections to several clauses in the proposed constitution. The first of these clauses empowered the national government to "make all laws" deemed necessary and proper for executing the powers vested in the national government under the Constitution. The second clause declared that all laws passed and all treaties signed by the national government were to be "the *supreme law* of the land; any thing in the constitution or laws of any State to the contrary notwithstanding." Anti-ratificationists cited these clauses as "pernicious engines by which their local governments were to be destroyed and their liberties exterminated."

Hamilton dismissed such views as gross "misrepresentation." Power was the ability or faculty of doing a thing, and the ability to do a thing rested on the power to employ means necessary for its execution. This was true in the matter of laying and collecting taxes: though a law laying a tax for the use of the United States would be a supreme law that could not legally be opposed or controlled, yet a law preventing the states from collecting a tax would not be supreme law because it would be unconstitutional.

Chapter 34 (Hamilton)

This essay takes up the subject of "CONCURRENT JURISDICTION" in the matter of taxes. Under the proposed constitution, the right of the national government to raise necessary revenues would be "altogether unlimited," while the revenue-raising power of individual states would be only moderately circumscribed under the plan of concurrent jurisdiction. Each would have its field, and there would not be any "sacrifice of the great INTERESTS of the Union to the POWER of the individual States."

Chapter 35 (Hamilton)

Hamilton posed a question here: what if the national government, as some proposed, should be empowered to raise revenue only through customs duties on foreign imports and exports? In want of any other source of revenue, such duties would undoubtedly have to be raised higher and higher. This would encourage smuggling to the detriment of law-abiding merchants and other businessmen. Higher tariffs would bring higher prices on many essentials and would adversely affect consumers. Protected by a high tariff wall, domestic manufacturers would enjoy an improper and "premature monopoly of the markets," which would unbalance the economy at the expense of other interests.

The idea of *actual* representation of all classes and interests in the legislature was "altogether visionary," said Hamilton. It was impossible to have members of each different trade and occupation seated in the legislature. Nor did mechanics and others wish to be seated. In general, such people were inclined to cast their votes for merchants, knowing "that the merchant is their natural patron and friend. . . . We must therefore consider merchants as the natural representatives of all these classes of the community."

All landowners, "from the wealthiest landlord to the poorest tenant," had one bond between them — to keep taxes on land as low as possible. So what did it matter whom they chose to represent them, whether "men of large fortunes or of moderate property or of no property at all"? From all of the above Hamilton concluded that the spirit of government would be best served if legislatures were composed, as most were, "of land-holders, merchants, and men of the learned professions," by which he meant lawyers in particular.

Chapter 36 (Hamilton)

The author continued to develop his thesis that, in the political nature of things, the national legislatures, like the state legislatures, would consist almost entirely of landowners, merchants, and members of the learned professions, who would "truly represent" the desires and interests of all the different classes and groups in the community.

It had been objected, Hamilton noted, that the national government's power of internal taxation could not be exercised with advantage from lack of sufficient knowledge of local circumstances. That supposition was "entirely destitute of foundation." All that was required of "inquisitive and enlightened Statesmen" was a general acquaintance with the resources and the different kinds of wealth, property, and industry in various parts of the country.

Also, in collecting internal taxes, the national government could make use of the tax apparatus already operating in the individual states. This would avoid the need for double sets of revenue officers and "duplication of their burthens by double taxations," which the people might resent. State revenue officers could be attached closely to the union by having the national government supplement their salaries.

As to poll taxes, which were in force in many states, Hamilton confessed his "disappointments" in them, adding that he would "lament to see them introduced into practice under the national government." On the other hand, the national government should have the power to impose poll taxes in case of need, for such taxes could become an "inestimable resource" of revenue for the nation as a whole.

COMMENTARIES

Chapters 30-36

Hamilton's ideas about a proper national tax structure are interesting, especially in view of the fact that he soon began putting them in effect when President Washington appointed him our first secretary of the treasury.

In this section of essays, Hamilton was ingenious, if not always convincing, in arguing his main thesis that the national government, as proposed under the new constitution, should have "altogether unlimited" authority to levy taxes on all things, and in whatever ways it thought best. But the government should use prudence and caution in exercising that authority.

Anti-Federalists objected that such blanket authority would place the states and the general public at the mercy of the national government. Hamilton denied this, saying that the authority would be exercised by the people's representatives in the Congress who could be trusted to act with discretion. If one set of representatives did not, the people could elect another set. But this, as Hamilton failed to mention, was easier said than done.

Few disagreed with Hamilton's view that, in the beginning at least, national revenues should come largely from "external" taxes (customs duties) and "internal" taxes in the form of excises on specified articles. Hamilton suggested that an excise on the making of "ardent spirits" would be not only profitable but socially desirable, for it would tend to curb the drinking of hard liquor, notoriously a "national extravagance." In one of his first acts at the Treasury, Hamilton proposed and Congress approved an excise tax on makers of "ardent spirits," which soon led to the Whiskey Rebellion by small distillers in western Pennsylvania and neighboring areas, a rebellion that Hamilton, as a major general, helped to put down.

Hamilton did rather well in explaining (Chapter 34) that no conflict could arise between the national government and the state governments about taxation because of "concurrent jurisdiction," a rather complicated concept. The national government's tax laws were to be the supreme law of the land, and not to be contravened in any way. At the same time the states would retain, with two minor exceptions, "independent and un-controlled" authority to levy taxes as they saw fit for their own purposes. The somewhat complex plan of "concurrent jurisdiction," it must be said, has worked rather well, with relatively little conflict or confusion.

Hamilton took a patrician view about the proper management of public affairs when he declared (Chapter 35) that the national legisla-ture not only would but should be composed predominantly of mer-chants, landowners, and men of the learned professions. These groups were experienced in large affairs and would "truly represent" all classes and interests in the country, said Hamilton, who went on to ask several rhetorical questions: would not the landholder know best how to pro-mote the interests of all landed property, large and small? Would not the merchant be disposed to cultivate, "as far as may be proper," the interests of the mechanic and manufacturing groups with whom he did business? Would not the man of the learned professions, being neutral between contending economic groups, be ready to promote the general interests of society? Thus, everybody's interests and problems would be taken care of. This was the British concept of "virtual representation."

All of this may seem politically naive, but it was not. Hamilton believed in rule by a propertied elite and, throughout his career, worked to keep it that way.

SECTION VI, CHAPTERS 37-40
DIFFICULTIES IN FRAMING CONSTITUTION

This section of four chapters deals with a wide miscellany of subjects, some of which are touched on only briefly.

SUMMARIES

Chapter 37 (Madison)

It was a sad commentary on human affairs that public measures can rarely be investigated with a spirit of moderation, said Madison, who then proceeded to take critics of the Constitution sharply to task. Some critics were well-intentioned; others were not; still others were stubborn or ignorant, or both.

Delegates who had just recently met at Philadelphia in the Constitutional Convention had set themselves the goal of designing an institutional framework that would allow a strong central government ample power to perform its tasks while still paying due attention to "liberty, and to the republican form," two elements, as Madison noted, always difficult to mix in the right proportions.

The convention had had to start from scratch, having no good example to follow. Many different views had been represented at the convention. In the debates there had been many spirited contentions between the large states and the small, between the several geographical sections of the country, between rural interests and urban interests, between creditors and debtors, etc. It had been necessary to adjust and accommodate all major interests and views.

Of course, said Madison, the Constitution was not perfect. But instead of being criticized, it should be praised and supported for being as good as it was under the circumstances. Besides, provision had been made for amending it to make it better, once it was adopted — which should be at once.

Chapter 38 (Madison)

America was like a man who finds his illness growing steadily worse and calls in doctors. After examinations and consultations, the doctors agree on what should be done in an increasingly dangerous situation. As soon as some of the patient's friends hear of this, they come in and, without any knowledge of medicine, warn the sick man that the doctors' prescription will poison his constitution and probably cause his death.

America was "sensible of her malady" and had called for advice from knowledgeable men of its choice. Yet this advice was being challenged and rejected by some.

Madison then briefly considered the main objections to the proposed constitution. Some did not want it because it was not a confederation of states but a government of individuals. Others agreed that it should be a government over individuals, but not to the extent proposed. There were those disturbed because the constitution did not contain a Bill of Rights. This was a chief objection of the Anti-Federalists, a legitimate objection soon removed by passage of the first ten amendments, since known as our national Bill of Rights. It was based on Virginia's celebrated Declaration of Rights (1776) drafted almost wholly by the great George Mason, a determined Anti-Federalist.

Having listed other objections raised against the proposed constitution, Madison asked critics to consider what kind of a government they had had before. It was not necessary that the proposed constitution be perfect: it *would* provide better government than under the Articles of Confederation. If the proposed constitution was not perfect, "no man would refuse to give brass for silver or gold, because the latter had some alloy in it."

An energetic government under the new constitution could help greatly in speeding the development of the Western frontier country, "a mine of vast wealth to the United States, . . . a rich and fertile country, of an area equal to the inhabited extent of the United States," out of which could be cut a number of new states.

Chapter 39 (Madison)

The first question Madison offers here is whether the new national government would be "strictly republican" in form. No other form would be compatible "with the genius of the people of America; with the fundamental principles of the revolution."

Madison defined a republic as a government deriving all its powers from the great body of the people and administered by persons holding office during the people's pleasure for a limited period, or during good behavior. The government under the proposed constitution answered that description. The House of Representatives was to be elected immediately by the people; the Senate and the president, indirectly by the people. Even the judges along with all other important national officers were to be the choice, "though a remote choice," of the people themselves.

Many objected that the new government would not be federal in form, based on the sovereignty of the states, but rather a national government based on a "consolidation" of the states. Madison analyzed this objection at length, arguing that the new government would be at once a federal and national government—federal in most respects, but necessarily national in others.

Chapter 40 (Madison)

Had the Constitutional Convention at Philadelphia been "authorised to frame and propose this mixed Constitution"? Anti-Federalists said No. As expressed in a resolution by the Continental Congress, the convention had been called for the "sole and express purpose of *revising the articles of confederation*," and the Articles of Confederation, instead of being revised, had been entirely scrapped.

After arguing around this point at considerable length, Madison finally admitted that the delegates at the Constitutional Convention had exceeded their instructions, but were justified in doing so. Seeking to establish a more adequate central government, they had found that no mere revision of the Articles of Confederation would do. The foundation of the American government had to be changed.

Even if the drafting of a whole new constitution was unauthorized, said Madison, did it "follow that the Constitution ought, for that reason alone to be rejected? If . . . it be lawful to accept good advice even from an enemy, shall we set the ignoble example of refusing such advice even when it is offered by our friends" in the form of a new constitution "calculated to accomplish the views and happiness of the people of America"?

COMMENTARY

Chapters 37-40

Very little need be said here. Madison shared Washington and Hamilton's view that the proposed constitution, though not perfect, was the best that could be hoped for under the circumstances, and that provision had been made for means of amending it as faults appeared and necessity required.

It was a concession on Madison's part that he finally admitted that the delegates to the Constitutional Convention had violated their instructions: that they were merely to revise the Articles of Confederation. Instead, they had entirely scrapped them. Madison justified this in the name of the "higher good."

SECTION VII, CHAPTERS 41-46
GENERAL POWERS

This section of six chapters deals with most of the over-all powers to be granted to the national government under the proposed Constitution. The specific powers of the legislature, executive, and judiciary are discussed later.

SUMMARIES

Chapter 41 (Madison)

The proposed constitution should be considered from several general points of view. The first concerned the extent of power to be vested in the government.

In previous essays, Publius had already shown, said Madison, that extensive powers for the national government were "necessary means of attaining a necessary end." Critics kept contending that such extensive powers were too broad, unnecessary, inconvenient, and liable to abuse. Madison denied this.

Certainly, the national government should have unlimited power to raise armies and equip fleets for self-defense. Madison repeated Hamilton's argument that the country was so situated that a large standing army, an institution always dangerous to popular liberties, would not be necessary, so that the nation would not be "crushed between standing armies and perpetual taxes.... The power of regulating and calling forth the militia has been already sufficiently vindicated and explained."

It was also necessary that the national government have unlimited power in levying and borrowing money, as explained before. The government's revenue-raising power should not be restricted to "external" taxes alone, as many critics contended.

Chapter 42 (Madison)

The second general view of the proposed constitution should consider the government's power to regulate relations with foreign nations, i.e., to make treaties, to send and receive ambassadors and lesser diplomatic officers, to punish piracies and other felonies on the high seas, and to regulate foreign commerce, "including a power to prohibit the importation of slaves after the year 1808, and to lay an intermediate duty of ten dollars per head, as a discouragement to such importations."

It would have been well, said Madison, if the proposed constitution had ordered an immediate stop to the slave trade instead of putting it off till 1808. Even so, it was a "great point gained in favor of humanity, that a period of twenty years may terminate for ever . . . a traffic which has so long and so loudly upbraided the barbarism of modern policy" and that, in the interim, the government would considerably discourage that traffic.

Some critics, Madison noted, were attempting to pervert this provision into an objection against the Constitution by representing it, on the one hand, "as a criminal toleration of an illicit practice, and on the other, as calculated to prevent voluntary and beneficial emigrations from Europe to America." Such misinterpretations deserved no answer.

A third classification of the powers to be exercised by the proposed government came under the head of its authority to regulate commerce among the states and with Indian tribes, coin money, regulate its value and that of foreign currencies, provide for the punishment of counterfeiting, establish a standard of weights and measures, set up uniform rules for naturalization and bankruptcy, prescribe the manner in which all public records should be kept, and establish post offices and post roads. The desirability of giving the national government the power to do these things was obvious, said Madison, and needed no elaboration.

As to the power of regulating commerce among the states, and the prohibition that the states were not to erect tariff barriers against one another, this free interstate commerce would correct many inequities. Certain commercial states could no longer levy tribute on others. The Indian trade could be regulated better by the national government than by the individual states whose practices varied. The same was true of the rules of naturalization, for which the states had set varying and often conflicting standards.

Chapter 43 (Madison)

Madison listed nine powers, which he labeled "miscellaneous." The first on Madison's list, and one of the more interesting, was the power "to promote the progress of science and useful arts, by securing for a limited time, to authors and inventors, the exclusive right, to their respective writings and discoveries." Madison noted that the copyright of authors had long been judged to be a right under common law in Britain. Such copyrights, or patents, should be extended to protect and encourage inventors.

Another of the powers would be the national government's right to exclusive legislation over lands purchased from the states for the erection of forts, arsenals, dockyards, and other needful structures. Similar authority would be exercised over the district, not exceeding ten miles square, which was to be chosen as the seat of government, the national capital (later named the District of Columbia).

Other important miscellaneous powers included the right to define and punish treason, to admit new states into the union, to guarantee to every state a republican form of government, and to lay down the rules for amending the Constitution.

Chapter 44 (Madison)

A fifth classification of powers consisted of certain restrictions imposed on the authority of the states. No state was to enter into any treaty, alliance, or confederation; or coin money, issue bills of credit, pass any law impairing the obligation of contracts, "or grant any title of nobility." No state, without the consent of Congress, was to lay any imposts or duties on foreign imports and exports, or lay any duty on tonnage, or keep troops or ships of war in times of peace.

A sixth classification consisted of several powers and provisions designed to give effect to all the rest. One such provision gave the national government the power to make all laws deemed "necessary and proper for carrying into execution" all its other powers. No part of the proposed constitution, Madison observed, was being assailed "with more intemperance" by Anti-Federalists, who objected to the blanket phrase "necessary and proper." They wanted specifications. That was impossible, Madison replied. Had the Constitutional Convention attempted to specify the "particular" powers necessary for implementing the Constitution, that would have involved a "complete digest of laws on every subject to which the Constitution relates."

Taking higher ground, Madison declared: "No axiom is more clearly established in law, or in reason, than that wherever the end is required, the means are authorized; wherever a general power to do a thing is given, every particular power necessary for doing it, is included."

Another restriction on the states was salutary. As the measures adopted and the treaties signed by the national government were to be the supreme law of the land, that law was to be binding on all state judges, no matter what the constitution or laws of any state might be.

Also, the law requiring all federal officials to take an oath to support the Constitution was to be extended to include state officers and all members of state legislatures. State officials would be essential in giving effect to the federal Constitution. The election of the president and the United States Senate would depend in all cases upon the state legislatures.

Chapter 45 (Madison)

Would the powers of the national government be dangerous to the authority of the states? Critics said they would be; Madison said not. Under the Constitution, the states would retain a "very extensive portion of active sovereignty." Without the "intervention" of state legislatures, the president could not be elected. The United States Senate would be elected "absolutely and exclusively" by the state legislatures. The House of Representatives, though elected by the people, would be chosen very much under the influence of those men who had risen to become members of state legislatures.

The national government would employ far fewer persons than the state governments in the aggregate. Consequently, the personal influence of national employees would be less than that of state employees, who would also be closer to the people.

The powers to be delegated to the national government were few and defined, while those retained by the states were numerous and indefinite. The operations of the national government would be most extensive in times of war and danger; those of the states, in times of peace and security. The changes proposed in the constitution consisted "much less in the addition of NEW POWERS to the Union, than in the invigoration of its ORIGINAL POWERS." The regulation of interstate commerce was a new power, to be sure, but few seemed to object to that.

Chapter 46 (Madison)

The author next asked whether the national government or the state governments would have the advantage in gaining the support of the people. The state governments would, he argued, for they would take care of the more domestic and personal interests of the people. A greater number of individuals could expect to rise to office in state governments to enjoy the salaries and "emoluments" thereof.

If the national government ever became disposed to extend its power beyond due limits and raised a standing army to carry out its designs, that army, in relation to the total population, could not exceed 30,000 men. On the other hand, the combined militias of the states would total some 500,000 men, and American militiamen had proved what they could do by defeating British regulars during the Revolution. The states would have nothing to fear if they joined the union. There was no danger of state governments being annihilated.

COMMENTARY

Chapters 41-46

In this series of essays Madison was clear in his arguments that the new national government should have "unlimited" power in raising military forces for self-defense, in levying taxes and borrowing money, in dealing with foreign nations, in regulating interstate commerce and the Indian trade, in setting up uniform rules for naturalization and bankruptcy, and in establishing post offices, post roads, and other improvements.

In support of the provision that the new government should have the exclusive right to legislate for the national capital district (not yet designated), Madison declared (Chapter 43) that if it were otherwise, the "public authority might be insulted and its proceedings be interrupted, with impunity." As things have turned out, this provision was not a wise one. The residents of Washington, D.C., were deprived of the right to vote, even for municipal officers. (Congress still legislates for the city and as Congress directs its attention to national affairs, it has little time or disposition to deal with local affairs.)

Madison's defense (Chapter 44) of the Constitutional Convention's uninstructed action in scrapping the Articles of Confederation and drafting a whole new constitution was, to say the least, rather slippery and sophistical — quite at variance with the legal doctrine he had been preaching.

SECTION VIII, CHAPTERS 47-51
STRUCTURE OF NEW GOVERNMENT

This section of five essays deals largely with the question of establishing a proper and workable system of checks and balances between the several main departments, or branches, of government.

SUMMARIES

Chapters 47-48 (Madison)

The author declared that no political maxim was more important for liberty than that the legislative, executive, and judiciary departments should be separate and distinct. When all of these departments were in the same hands, "whether of one, a few or many, or whether hereditary, self appointed, or elective," that was the "very definition of tyranny." Critics of the Constitution contended that under it the separation of powers was vague and confusing.

Quoting Montesquieu's analysis of the British constitution, and citing the constitutions of various states, Madison argued that the three main branches of government could not be "totally separate and distinct" if they were to operate together as a whole.

Madison said that no main government branch should be directly administered by another, and that none should have an overruling influence over the others; how to obtain a proper balance between the three main departments of government was the problem. Detailing governmental operations under the constitutions of Virginia and Pennsylvania as an example, Madison concluded that the separation of powers was a "sacred maxim of free government," but the branches could not be "kept totally separate and distinct."

Madison then set out to demonstrate that the separate powers of the legislature, the executive, and the judiciary should be "so far connected and blended, as to give to each a constitutional controul over the others."

By its very nature, the legislative branch tended to gain a superiority over the two other branches. Its powers were at once broader and less susceptible to precise limits. Besides, it alone had "access to the pockets of the people." Having cited operations under the Virginia and Pennsylvania constitutions, Madison concluded that a mere definition on paper of the three departments' constitutional limits was not a sufficient guard against encroachments leading toward a "tyrannical concentration . . . in the same hands."

Chapter 49 (Madison)

This essay begins by quoting from Jefferson, who had declared that whenever any two of the three branches of government agreed that a convention should be called for amending the Constitution, "or *correcting breaches of it*," then such a convention should be called.

Publius agreed that this was strictly in accord with republican theory, but there were "insuperable objections" against frequent appeals to the people. For one thing, such appeals would imply defects in the government which would deprive it of "that veneration, which time bestows on every thing, and without which perhaps the wisest and freest governments would not possess the requisite stability." Frequent appeals would inflame public passions, for America was not a "nation of philosophers" able to discuss such questions in a cool and rational manner.

The greatest objection against frequent appeals to the people on constitutional questions was that this procedure would not maintain the government's constitutional equilibrium. The legislative branch, being the strongest, would probably be the most frequently charged with encroachments on the others. As the members of the executive and judiciary departments would be fewer in number and less known personally to the public, members of the legislative branch, having been chosen immediately by the people, would have the advantage in swinging public opinion to their point of view.

Frequent appeals to the people were not a proper or effective way of keeping the three main governmental departments within their prescribed constitutional limits.

Chapter 50 (Madison or Hamilton)

In place of "*occasional* appeals to the people" about constitutional questions, some were arguing for "*periodical* appeals" as an adequate means of preventing and correcting infractions of the Constitution.

This method would not work either. If the time between periodical appeals were made short, there would be the same objections as against occasional appeals. If the periods were made longer, it might well be that the abuses complained of would have taken such deep root that they could not easily be removed. Certain proceedings in Pennsylvania in 1783-84 were then cited to substantiate this point.

Chapter 51 (Madison or Hamilton)

The only way of assuring the separation of legislative, executive, and judicial powers was to contrive such an inner structure of government that the departments might, "by their mutual relations, be the means of keeping each other in their proper places."

Each department should have a will of its own, and its members should have no "agency" in appointing members of the others. Those administering each department should have the constitutional means and "personal motives to resist encroachments of the others." Publius continued:

> Ambition must be made to counteract ambition . . . It may be a reflection on human nature, that such devices should be necessary to controul the abuses of government. But what is government itself but the greatest of all reflections on human nature? If men were angels, no government would be necessary. . . . In framing a government . . . to be administered by men over men, the great difficulty lies in this: You must first enable the government to controul the governed; and, in the next place, oblige it to controul itself.

The proposed Constitution did just that—by so dividing and arranging the several offices that "each may be a check on the other; that the

the private interest of every individual, may be a sentinel over the public rights."

COMMENTARY

Chapters 47-51

This section is largely an elaboration on arguments made more briefly before. The only new matter introduced in this section consisted of the objections to occasional appeals to the people on constitutional questions, as advocated by Jefferson (Chapter 49), and the equal objections to periodical appeals (Chapter 50).

SECTION IX, CHAPTERS 52-61
HOUSE OF REPRESENTATIVES

This section of ten chapters deals in some detail with the structure and many powers of the lower house of Congress as proposed by the new Constitution.

SUMMARIES

Chapter 52 (Madison or Hamilton)

What should be the qualifications of the electors and the elected? The new Constitution laid it down that a representative in the House had to be twenty-five years old, a United States citizen for seven years, and a resident of the state he was representing. He would hold office for two years. Going back to colonial days, the states had fixed varying periods of election from one to seven years. It had seemed best to make the period uniform—an election for the House every two years.

Chapter 53 (Madison)

Some critics contended that elections to the House should be held annually, quoting the adage that "where annual elections end, tyranny begins."

Publius disputed this. A one-year term of office was too short. A House member would scarcely have time to learn his duties before he would be faced with the expense and time of standing for election again. Under such a circumstance, no representative could be expected to learn much about national affairs either in the domestic or foreign field.

Chapter 54 (Madison or Hamilton)

As the number of each state's delegates to the House was to be determined by the size of its population, were slaves to be included? The southern states considered their slaves "in some degree as men." In a compromise, the Constitution stipulated that slaves should be counted as inhabitants, but because of their servitude each was to be counted as only three-fifths of a man.

Chapter 55 (Madison or Hamilton)

It was argued against the House of Representatives that, in the beginning at least, it would have too few members to be a safe "depository of the public interests," and could not be trusted with so much power.

The states varied greatly in the number of delegates they had in the lower houses of their legislative assemblies. Under the proposed constitution, the number of seats in the House of Representatives at the beginning would be sixty-five. But a census was to be taken within three years, and it might raise the number of representatives to one hundred. It was estimated that, with population growth, the number would be two hundred in twenty-five years, and four hundred in fifty years, which should put an end to all fears about the small size of the body.

Chapter 56 (Madison or Hamilton)

It was also charged that the House of Representatives would be too small to have adequate knowledge of the interests of its constituents.

Representatives should know the needs of their constituents and be responsive to them, of course, but they should have time in office to acquire some perspective on such national problems as regulation of foreign and interstate commerce, taxation, defense, etc. A House representing every 30,000 inhabitants in the country would be "both a safe and competent guardian of the interests . . . confided to it."

Chapter 57 (Madison or Hamilton)

Another charge against the House of Representatives was that it would be composed of those with least sympathy for the mass of the people and most likely "to aim at an ambitious sacrifice of the many to the aggrandizement of the few." This would depend on who was entitled to vote for the representatives.

Who *were* to be the electors of the federal representatives? They were to be the same as those who elected representatives to the lower legislative chambers in the various states. The electors would be the great body of the American people: "not the rich more than the poor; not the learned more than the ignorant; not the haughty heirs of distinguished names, more than the humble sons of obscure and unpropitious fortune." Such electors could be trusted to choose fitting public-spirited persons to represent them and their various interests in the House of Representatives.

Chapter 58 (Madison or Hamilton)

Critics of the Constitution were contending that no assurance was given that the number of members in the House would increase with the growth in population.

That was a mistaken view. It was stipulated that within three years, in 1790, a population census was to be taken, and a similar census every ten years thereafter, to determine what adjustments should be made in the number of each state's representatives in the House. There would be small chance of organized resistance to such adjustments, for the people would demand changes to secure adequate representation.

Chapter 59 (Hamilton)

The new Constitution provided that the time, place, and manner of electing United States senators and representatives should be regulated by the state legislatures, but that the Congress could alter such regulations, "except as to *places* of choosing senators."

This provision had been attacked, but nothing was more evident than the "plain proposition, that *every government ought to contain in itself the means of its own preservation.*" If the power of regulating elections for the national government were left entirely in the hands of state legislatures, the latter would have the union entirely at their mercy, and might take off on various divergences and obstructions.

Chapter 60 (Hamilton)

What would be the danger if the ultimate right of regulating its own elections were left to the union itself? There should be no apprehension on that score. That provision could not be used "to promote the election of some favourite class of men in exclusion of others." There would be no possibility of domination by the "wealthy and the well born," as critics contended. Agriculture and commerce, the landed interests and the mercantile interests, would have weight in national councils proportionate to their strength in the several states, with the bulk of the voters having a predominant voice in each state.

Chapter 61 (Hamilton)

Hamilton replied to the objection that had been raised that elections were not, by law, required to be held in the counties where the voters resided. He cited the practices in New York, noting that while the objection had some validity, it was not very important. More important was the provision in the Constitution that there should be uniformity in the times of periodically electing members to the House of Representatives and the United States Senate. Such uniformity would be of great benefit to the public welfare, "both as a security against . . . the same spirit in the body; and as a cure for the diseases of faction."

COMMENTARY

Chapters 52-61

No comment is needed on this section, which is simply an exposition and justification of the provisions in the proposed constitution about the House of Representatives: qualifications of members, by whom elected, and tenure of office.

SECTION X, CHAPTERS 62-66
UNITED STATES SENATE

This section follows the pattern of the previous section, and is concerned with the qualifications and powers of the Senate.

SUMMARIES

Chapter 62 (Madison or Hamilton)

Qualifications for senators were these: they had to be at least thirty years old, and to have been citizens of the nation for nine years. They were to be designated by the elected legislatures of the individual states. Senators would hold office for six years, but under a rotation system whereby one-third of the body would be up for election every two years.

At any one time, therefore, two-thirds of the Senate would consist of experienced members, which would give stability and continuity to the Senate's deliberations and decisions.

In the Senate, unlike the House, the states would have equal representation; each state, no matter how large or how small, would have two senators. Brought about by a compromise, this was a "constitutional recognition of the portion of sovereignty remaining in the individual states." This arrangement would empede passage of bad legislation. No law or resolution could be passed "without the concurrence first of a majority of the people [speaking through the House of Representatives], and then of a majority of the states [speaking through the Senate]."

Chapter 63 (Madison or Hamilton)

The stability and wisdom of such a select Senate would do much to gain the United States more respect from foreign nations. Examples from the history of the republics of antiquity supported this view.

Chapter 64 (Jay)

The proposed constitution would give the president the power to make treaties, *"by and with the advice and consent of the senate,"* provided that two-thirds of the senators present concurred.

This proviso was a wise one. The method of electing senators, and the president, would ensure that direction of foreign affairs would be exercised by men "most distinguished by their abilities and virtue, and in whom the people perceive just grounds for confidence.... With such men the power of making treaties may be safely lodged." That power could not be safely entrusted to popular assemblies such as the House of Representatives, subject to drastic changes every two years.

To suppose that "corruption" might influence the president *and* two-thirds of the Senate in making treaties was an idea "too gross and too invidious to be entertained."

Chapter 65 (Hamilton)

The proposed constitution gave the Senate the power to participate with the executive in the appointment of major national officers, and to act as a court in impeachment trials. By its character and composition the Senate was well fitted to initiate, prosecute, and judge impeachment proceedings, acting as a "bridle" on those exercising executive powers.

Chapter 66 (Hamilton)

The Senate would sit as a jury after the House had passed a motion for impeachment. A two-thirds majority in favor of conviction would be required in the Senate; that would provide ample "security to innocence," and there would be no danger of persecutions.

As proposed in the Constitution, the president would nominate men for government office and appoint them "with the advice and consent of the senate." But the Senate would have no voice in choosing nominees. If it disapproved of a particular nominee, the Senate could reject him and force the president to name another, thus having the power to exercise a veto on major appointments.

COMMENTARY

Chapters 62-66

As this section is largely expository, detailing the nature and necessity of the powers to be exercised by the United States Senate, there is no need to comment except perhaps to note this: Publius made much of the "distinctive" character of the Senate arising from the fact that its members would be chosen by the state legislatures, and not directly by the people, as was the case with members of the House of Representatives. In 1913, with the adoption of the Seventeenth Amendment to the Constitution, it was stipulated that United States Senators in each state were to be "elected by the people thereof."

SECTION XI, CHAPTERS 67-77
NEED FOR A STRONG EXECUTIVE

This group of eleven essays discusses and defends, one by one, the extensive powers to be bestowed on the president under the proposed constitution.

SUMMARIES

Chapter 67 (Hamilton)

No part of the proposed constitution had been more difficult to arrange than that dealing with the executive, and no part was being "inveighed against with less candor, or criticised with less judgment," Hamilton protested.

Critics were playing on the "aversion of the people to monarchy." Some were picturing the intended president as having the power to make himself a despot, "with the diadem sparkling on his brow, and the imperial purple flowing in his train. . . . seated on a throne surrounded with minions and mistresses." Some had gone so far in imagination as to equip him with a harem.

Critics contended that the Constitution gave the president power to fill vacancies in the United States Senate. That was not true, Hamilton pointed out. The power to fill temporary vacancies in the Senate was "expressly" allotted to the executives in the individual states.

As to making appointments to vacancies in major government posts while the Senate was in recess, the president would have the power to fill such vacancies by granting temporary commissions, such commissions to run only to the end of the next Senate session. By that time, hopefully, the Senate would have considered and either approved or disapproved of such commissions. There was here no danger of presidential power-grabbing.

Chapter 68 (Hamilton)

The way of electing a president, Hamilton noted with relief, was "almost the only part of the system, of any consequence, which has escaped without severe censure."

Rightly, the "sense of the people should operate in the choice" of the chief executive. But this was to be accomplished in a special way. Instead of committing the election of the president to any established body, the choice should be made by men chosen for the special purpose, and meeting at particular times. Such men of distinction would be the most capable of deciding which presidential candidate had the best qualifications for office.

Under the plan, each state was to choose a number of electors equal to the state's number of senators and representatives in the national government. The electors would meet in each state and transmit their decision to the national government. A candidate had to obtain a majority of votes in the electoral college to be named president. In case there was not a majority, provision had been made to have the choice determined by the House of Representatives, in which each state was to have only one vote. How each state voted as a unit was to be determined, presumably, by a caucus taken among the state's delegates to the House.

A vice president was also to be elected by the electoral college. He was to be the candidate who received the next highest vote after the president-elect. Among his other duties, he was to be *ex officio* the presiding officer in the United States Senate, entitled to vote only to break a deadlock in the Senate when the vote on a particular measure was tied.

Chapter 69 (Hamilton)

The president would be elected for a term of four years; he would be eligible for re-election. He would not have the life tenure of an hereditary monarch. The president would be liable to impeachment, trial, and removal from office upon being found guilty of treason, bribery, or other high crimes and misdemeanors. He would be accountable at all times to the country at large.

The president was also to be the commander-in-chief of all regular United States military forces and of the state militias when called into national service. The president would have only occasional command of the state militias, and only when authorized by the Congress.

In addition, the president would have the power to pardon all offenders except those found guilty in an impeachment trial. He would regulate foreign relations with the advice and consent of the Senate, and have other extensive powers. But since a president was to be elected every four years, he could not possibly become a "perpetual and *hereditary* prince" like the despised and "tyrannical" King George III of Britain.

Chapter 70 (Hamilton)

There were some who argued that a vigorous executive was inconsistent with republican principles. All men of sense agreed, said Hamilton, about the "necessity of an energetic executive." That necessary energy would come from unity, duration, adequate provision for its support, and competent powers. The first need was "due dependence on the people"; the second, due responsibility.

As to unity, Hamilton argued (largely to himself), that executive powers should be concentrated in a single chief magistrate, and not in a council or anything of that sort. The history of Rome and the ancient Greek republics proved this, as well as the operations under various state governments. As chief magistrate, the president should bear sole responsibility for his acts. There was no need of a "council to the executive."

Chapter 71 (Hamilton)

This is a prolix essay on why the president's term in office should be limited and why a new election to the presidency should be held periodically: every four years, as proposed. Four years would be long enough, but not too long. That period would keep the president responsive to the changing views and interests of the people if he hoped for re-election.

Chapter 72 (Hamilton)

The president should be eligible for re-election. Otherwise, the chief magistrate might become irresponsible. Knowing that he would not be called to account by the people for whatever he did, he might do whatever he pleased, making himself a fortune while he could.

A man having served four years as president would have more knowledge of statecraft and the inner workings of the government than one who had not. To exclude a president from seeking to succeed himself might well result in the "fatal inconveniences of fluctuating councils and a variable policy."

Chapter 73 (Hamilton)

The vigor of the executive branch depended on adequate provision for its support, to be determined by Congress. It was possible that Congress might decide to "starve" an unpopular president by reducing or abolishing his salary, or "tempt him by largesses" to surrender his judgment and discretion.

No provision in the proposed constitution was more "judicious" than this, said Hamilton: the president would receive for his services a compensation *"which shall neither be increased nor diminished, during the period for which he shall have been elected, . . .* and shall *not receive within that period any other emolument* from the United States or any of them." This would make the president financially independent and free to move as his judgment dictated.

The president should have the power to exercise a qualified negative over the acts of the two legislative bodies. He could return all bills he objected to so that they could not become laws unless subsequently passed again, this time by a two-thirds vote in both houses of Congress. This would protect the president from having his powers whittled away by the legislature, and be a safeguard against hasty and ill-considered legislation. This would tend toward greater stability in government. To avoid a clash with the legislature, the president would be inclined to use his qualified veto cautiously.

Chapter 74 (Hamilton)

Among other requisite powers, the president was to be commander-in-chief of all regular United States military forces and of the state militias *"when called into the actual service of the United States."* The propriety and reasons for this were so obvious, said Hamilton, that there was no need to discuss them.

The president was to have the power to grant pardons and reprieves for offences against the United States, *"except in cases of impeachment."* There had been little criticism of this, Hamilton noted, except in relation to treason. Some argued that one or both legislative houses should be brought into proceedings involving the possible pardon of anyone convicted of treason. Hamilton saw some merit in that view, but concluded by saying that the power of granting pardons in treason cases should be left solely in the hands of the president, for "in seasons of insurrection or rebellion" the president could act more decisively and judiciously in granting amnesties. This might prevent the contending groups from coming to a violent and possibly disastrous collision.

Chapter 75 (Hamilton)

In the author's opinion, "one of the best digested and most unexceptionable parts" of the Constitution was the provision empowering the president to make treaties, but only "by and with the advice and consent of the senate . . . provided two-thirds of the senators present concur."

This would prevent an irresponsible president, whether from ambition, or avarice, or other motive, from negotiating and signing a treaty without due consideration. No treaty could go into effect until the Senate had discussed and debated it and given approval by a two-thirds vote.

A few minor objections had been raised to this provision. Some argued that approval in the Senate should not depend on a two-thirds vote of senators present, but on a two-thirds vote based on the entire membership of the Senate, which might be entirely different. Hamilton dismissed this argument as academic. The votes on this question should be those of the senators present, those who had taken pains to make sure that they would be present. For good reasons and bad, senators would often be absent on critical roll calls.

It had also been argued that the House of Representatives should "share in the formation of treaties." Hamilton replied that the members of the House were too many and too diverse in their interests, that their two-year term of office was too short to expect of them any "accurate and comprehensive knowledge of foreign politics."

Chapter 76 (Hamilton)

With the advice and consent of the Senate, the president was to have the power to nominate and appoint ambassadors, other public ministers, justices of the Supreme Court, and all other United States officers. However, Congress could, by law, "vest the appointment of such inferior officers as they think proper in the President alone, or in the Courts of law, or in the heads of departments."

Hamilton repeated what he had previously said, that the "true test of a good government is its aptitude and tendency to produce a good administration." Surely, he said, almost everyone would agree that the proposed plan for making appointments would "produce a judicious choice" of men for filling offices. The president would have the sole responsibility of nominating men for higher office, but there was a check on him. His nominees could be rejected by the Senate, which would greatly tend to prevent the appointment of "unfit characters."

Chapter 77 (Hamilton)

Cooperation of the Senate in the matter of appointments would add to the stability of the administration. As the consent of the Senate would be necessary to displace as well as to appoint, a change of president would not occasion "so violent or so general a revolution in the officers of the government . . . if he were the sole disposer of offices." If a man had proved his fitness in any particular high office, a new president would hesitate to displace him and bring in someone "more agreeable to him" from fear of getting a rebuff in the Senate which would "bring some degree of discredit upon himself."

After arguing at some length (and more than a bit tediously) on the point that such an arrangement would not give the president "improper influence" over the Senate, nor the Senate over the president, Hamilton enumerated the remaining powers of the president, the chief being these: giving information to Congress on the state of the union, recommending to Congress what measures he judged to be necessary or expedient, and calling Congress into special session on extraordinary occasions.

He hoped he had demonstrated, said Publius, that the structure and powers of the executive department combined, "as far as republican principles would admit, all the requisites to energy." There was one more major consideration about the proposed constitution: "Does it also combine the requisites to safety in the republican sense — a due dependence on the people — a due responsibility?"

COMMENTARIES

Chapter 67

Hamilton was right in observing that no part of the proposed constitution was being more severely criticized than the broad strong powers to be exercised by the executive. The popular and fiery Patrick Henry, perhaps the most influential leader of the opposition, spoke for a large number of thoughtful men in saying of the Constitution that, "among other deformities, it has an awful squinting — it squints toward monarchy. And does not this raise indignation in the breast of every true American? Your president may easily become King. . . . Where are your checks in this government?"

Incidentally, as evidence of widespread monarchical leanings, an organized movement had already proposed that Washington declare himself king, a suggestion that Washington angrily denounced.

Hamilton failed to mention another major objection to the Constitution, either here or later. The strong powers of the national government were spelled out at length, but there was not a word about the rights of states and the liberties of individuals. There was no Bill of Rights guaranteeing religious freedom, liberty of the press, the right of popular assembly, trial by jury, and other "sacred rights." Anti-Federalists took a strong stand that the proposed constitution should not be adopted until it had been revised to include a Bill of Rights. It was the possibility that the Philadelphia document might be sent back for revisions that most frightened the Federalists. They had convinced themselves that adoption of the present draft was of vital necessity.

Anti-Federalists made a strong case and soon won their point. One of the first acts of the new national government was passage of the first ten amendments to the Constitution, our long (and rightly) celebrated Bill of Rights, increasingly the heart of our democratic society. The amendments were largely drafted and pushed to adoption by Madison, who soon became an Anti-Federalist, joining with Jefferson in putting together varied groups in the first organized opposition, the Republican-Democratic party.

Chapter 68

Hamilton's high praise of the electoral college system of electing a president is interesting, particularly in view of the current growing feeling that the electoral college system should be abolished entirely as cumbersome, irrelevant, and potentially dangerous. Most of those who take that view seem to favor a plan whereby the president would be elected by direct popular vote, as in the case of governors, mayors, legislative members, and all other elected officials.

Chapters 69-74

No comment is needed here on Hamilton's outline of what a president's powers should be, or the duration of his term in office. But this should be noted: a president was to be elected every four years, and was eligible for re-election. There was no constitutional restriction on how many times he might succeed himself; he might go on indefinitely.

After two terms, President Washington stepped down, establishing a two-term precedent that was followed until it was broken by President Franklin D. Roosevelt in 1940, and again in 1944. That will not happen again. A constitutional amendment (XXII) now limits a president's tenure to two terms, with one exception: if he should succeed to the office following the death or removal of the president, and serve less than two years of that term, he may then be *elected* for an additional two terms.

Chapters 75-77

In these chapters Hamilton does well in elaborating on many great advantages to flow from the constitutional provisions encouraging and facilitating close co-operation between the president and the legislature, especially with the Senate, on such important matters as making treaties, making major appointments, and seating Supreme Court justices, among other things.

SECTION XII, CHAPTERS 78-83
JUDICIARY

This section of six chapters deals with the proposed structure of federal courts, their powers and jurisdiction, the method of appointing judges, and related matters.

SUMMARIES

Chapter 78 (Hamilton)

A first important consideration was the manner of appointing federal judges, and the length of their tenure in office. They should be appointed in the same way as other federal officers, which had been discussed before. As to tenure, the Constitution proposed that they should hold office *"during good behaviour,"* a provision to be found in the consitutions of almost all the states. As experience had proved, there was no better way of securing a steady, upright, and impartial administration of the law. To perform its functions well, the judiciary had to remain "truly distinct" from both the legislative and executive branches of the government, and act as a check on both.

There had been some question—Hamilton called it a "perplexity," as well he might—about the rights of the courts to declare a legislative act null and void if, in the court's opinion, it violated the Constitution. It was argued that this implied a "superiority of the judiciary to the legislative power." Not at all, Hamilton argued. The courts had to regard the Constitution as fundamental law, and it was, therefore, the responsibility of the courts "to ascertain its meaning as well as the meaning of any particular act proceeding from the legislative body." The same should apply to actions taken by the executive.

Chapter 79 (Hamilton)

Nothing contributed more to the independence of judges than a "fixed provision for their support." Hamilton repeated here what he had said in regard to the executive, that "in the general course of human nature, *a power over a man's subsistence amounts to a power over his will.*" The Constitution therefore wisely proposed that the salaries of federal judges could "not be *diminished* during their continuance in office," though they might be increased at the discretion of Congress.

There should be no provision for removing judges because of alleged "inability," except in cases of insanity. Nor should there be any mandatory age for retirement. Older and more experienced judges were very often the better ones.

Chapter 80 (Hamilton)

As to the jurisdiction of the federal courts, they should have the authority to overrule state laws contravening the Constitution. They should have the power to enforce uniformity in the interpretation of national laws. They should have jurisdiction in all cases involving citizens of other nations.

And most important in assuring domestic order and tranquillity, federal courts should have jurisdiction in conflicts between the states, such as on boundary disputes. They should have jurisdiction in determining causes between one state and the citizens of another, and between the citizens of different states. Only federal courts could impartially judge such cases. The national judiciary should also have jurisdiction in maritime cases, for the latter often involved the rights of foreigners, rights assured to them by treaties which were *per se* part of the supreme law of the land.

Chapter 81 (Hamilton)

Under the proposed constitution, judicial power was to be vested "in one supreme court, and in such inferior courts as the congress may from time to time ordain and establish."

All agreed on the necessity of one supreme court with final jurisdiction, but some took the view that it should not constitute a separate branch of government. Rather, it should be a branch of the legislature since it would be "construing" laws. In Britain, for example, the court of last resort was the House of Lords, a legislative body, a feature that had been imitated in the constitutions of a number of states.

On this point Hamilton replied that members of the legislature were not chosen primarily for their qualifications to sit as judges, and were always subject to party divisions, so that the "pestilential breath of faction may poison the fountains of justice."

As to the power of instituting inferior federal courts, this would enable the national government to authorize in every state or sizeable district a tribunal competent to deal with matters of national jurisdiction. The inferior federal courts would be a screen, as it were, to keep all cases involving federal law from going directly to the Supreme Court. Many cases could be satisfactorily adjudicated in the lower courts.

Some were asking why the same purpose could not be accomplished by using already established state courts, without elaborating federal machinery. Hamilton admitted that there were several different answers to this.

State courts, of course, should be allowed the utmost latitude in the field of their jurisdiction. But they were not competent to sit in judgment on national laws and interpretations of the Constitution. Their decisions might often have a state bias. But the Constitution would not trample on the rights and powers of state courts, or county courts, within the limits of their jurisdiction.

Chapter 82 (Hamilton)

This is a legalistic essay, to be easily understood only by a lawyer, on the complex "doctrine of concurrent jurisdiction" between the national and the state courts. The doctrine involved the question of which courts had primary jurisdiction, and how appeals would be made from court to court.

Having cited a number of hypothetical examples, Hamilton concluded that as state governments and the national government were kindred systems and "parts of ONE WHOLE," the inference was conclusive that state courts would have concurrent jurisdiction in all cases arising under federal law, except where "expressly prohibited."

Chapter 83 (Hamilton)

Objection had been raised that the constitution contained no specific provision for trial by jury in civil cases. In this lengthy essay Hamilton argued that because the constitution did not specifically provide for trial by jury in civil cases, this did not mean that the right to such a trial was entirely abolished.

Hamilton went on to point out that in regard to this right there was no uniformity in the constitutions and laws of the various states. Nor was it desirable to enforce such uniformity by national law. Critics contended that trial by jury in all cases was the "very palladium of free government."

For his part, said Hamilton, "I must acknowledge that I cannot readily discern the inseparable connection between the existence of liberty and the trial by jury in civil cases. . . . I feel a deep and deliberate conviction, that there are many cases in which the trial by jury is an ineligible one. . . . The best judges of the matter will be the least anxious for a constitutional establishment of the trial by jury in civil cases."

COMMENTARIES

Chapter 78

In this essay Hamilton discussed the question of whether the Supreme Court should have the authority to declare acts of Congress null and void because, in the Court's opinion, they violated the Constitution. Hamilton answered in the affirmative; such a power would tend to curb the "turbulence and follies of democracy." But others have disagreed with Hamilton about this. Among those who have wished to curtail the Supreme Court's power to invalidate acts of Congress have been Presidents Jefferson, Jackson, Lincoln, Theodore Roosevelt, and Franklin D. Roosevelt. The issue is still a live one, as is evident from the heated debates of recent years.

Chapter 79

In arguing that the independence of judges could only be assured by making a fixed provision for their support, Hamilton made a profound and realistic social observation: "In the general course of human nature, *a power over a man's subsistence amounts to a power over his will.*" This is as true of private as of public life.

Chapter 80

This essay on why the United States Supreme Court should have the authority to overrule state laws which in its judgment contravened the Constitution, and to enforce uniformity in the interpretation of national laws, is self-explanatory. Was there to be a national law, or not? If so desired, there was only one way to accomplish this.

Chapter 81

Hamilton made a convincing argument here against the objection that there should be no inferior federal courts, on the grounds that this would undermine and usurp the authority of state courts. Why not let state courts handle federal questions arising within their jurisdictions? Because, said Hamilton, state courts would be likely to be state-biased or regionally oriented in judging national issues.

Chapter 82

In this essay Hamilton did reasonably well in clarifying for the lay mind the perplexities about how the highly legalistic "doctrine of concurrent jurisdiction" between national and state courts would work in practice.

Chapter 83

This essay is rather specious in its argument against the objection that the proposed Constitution contained no specific provision for trial by jury in civil cases. The Constitution stipulated that anyone indicted on a criminal charge had the right, if he chose to exercise it, to be tried by a jury. But nothing was said about civil cases. The fact that nothing was said did not mean the right to jury trial in civil cases was entirely abolished, said Hamilton. "Every man of discernment must at once perceive the wide difference between *silence* and *abolition*." But many men of high discernment, including some leading Federalists, saw a wide difference, thought the silence ominous, and were uneasy about it.

SECTION XIII, CHAPTERS 84, 85
CONCLUSIONS

The two chapters in this section pick up, and in places extend, the arguments made before. Nothing materially new is added in these chapters. For obvious reasons, summary and commentary have been combined here.

Chapter 84 (Hamilton)

This essay first takes up the objection that the proposed constitution contained no Bill of Rights. To this Hamilton replied that the constitutions of many states (including his own, New York) contained no specific bill of rights.

Hamilton then proceeded to beg the question by citing what rights were guaranteed under the Constitution—judgment in impeachment cases should not involve more than removal from office; all trials, except in cases of impeachment, would be held by jury; the writ of *habeas corpus* was not to be suspended except in cases of invasion or insurrection where public safety required it; no titles of nobility were to be granted. "Nothing need be said to illustrate the importance of the prohibition of titles of nobility. This may truly be denominated the corner stone of republican government" said Hamilton.

As an argument, this was ridiculous and diversive. What average Americans wanted to know was what constitutional guarantees they would have to enjoy freedom of religion, liberty of the press, freedom of speech, the right of people to assemble peaceably and to petition the government for redress of grievances, the right of individuals to keep and bear arms, the right of all people "to be secure in their persons, houses, papers, and effects against unreasonable searches and seizures." These rights were soon stated concretely, and adopted as the first ten amendments to the Constitution.

To his credit, let it be said, Madison promised that, if elected to the new Congress, he would use his every effort to see that, as a first order of business, a Bill of Rights was appended to the Constitution, and he carried out his pledge. As noted earlier, it was Madison who largely drafted the amendments and did the political engineering that brought about their adoption.

As for Hamilton, he stated explicitly in this essay that a Bill of Rights was not only unnecessary in the proposed constitution, "but would even be dangerous" — another reflection of his deep-grained anti-democratic attitudes.

The essay next replied to the objection (a minor one) that the seat of the national government, wherever placed, would be far from many parts of the country and the people there would have difficulty in keeping track of what was going on. Well, said Hamilton, if there was to be a national capital, it had to be located somewhere, and the people in more distant parts had ample means of communication and sources of information to enable them to check up on what their representatives were doing in the capital.

On another point, it was being argued that the establishment of a national government would entail additional expense and higher taxes. This would not be so, at least not in the beginning. The national government would take over the expense of performing functions and maintaining offices that the states were already supporting by requisitions made upon them under the Articles of Confederation. It would be merely a change of paymasters entailing no additional expense except in one respect. Support of the proposed new national judicial system would entail a small extra expense, but it was well worth it.

Chapter 85 (Hamilton)

There remained two more points to be discussed: the analogy of the proposed constitution "to your own state constitution" (the Federalist papers, as noted before, were all addressed "to the People of the State of New York"), and the additional security which its adoption would afford "to republican government, to liberty and to property."

The New York State constitution contained as many "supposed defects," and many of the same kind, as those complained about in the proposed national constitution, and yet no great clamor had been raised about these.

Additional securities to republican government, liberty, and property under the proposed constitution would come chiefly "in the restraints which the preservation of the union will impose on local factions and insurrections . . . in the diminution of the opportunities to foreign intrigue . . . in the prevention of extensive military establishments . . . in the absolute and universal exclusion of titles of nobility; and in the precautions against the repetition of those practices on the part of the state governments, which have undermined the foundations of property and credit."

Certainly the proposed constitution was not a perfect thing, but it should be accepted as it was without prior modifications and amendments. The plan was the best that could be expected under the circumstances. Provision had been made for amending it later.

In an exhortatory conclusion, Publius (speaking through Hamilton) declared that all sincere friends of the union should be on guard "against hazarding anarchy, civil war, a perpetual alienation of the states from each other, and perhaps the military despotism of a victorious demagogue. . . . A NATION without a NATIONAL GOVERNMENT is, in my view, an awful spectacle."

No attempt should be made to revise the proposed Constitution. "I dread the more the consequences of new attempts, because I KNOW that POWERFUL INDIVIDUALS, in this and in other states, are enemies to a general national government, in every possible shape."

This was special pleading, and not true. Many venerable patriots of greater stature and longer standing than Hamilton at the time – Patrick Henry, George Mason, Richard Henry Lee, Governor George Clinton of New York, Sam Adams of Massachusetts, among others – did not object to a national government, but raised fundamental questions about whether the proposed constitution was as well designed as it might be to achieve that end.

REVIEW QUESTIONS

At the outset, certain terms have to be clearly understood (use of a large reference work will help clarify definitions and shades of meaning).

1. What, essentially, is the difference between a federal government and a confederation of states? Between a republic and a democracy? What is the meaning of "anarchy" by strict definition? And by loose definition, the form commonly used?

2. To get an idea of the structure and scope of the book, review the outline (Chapter 1) of the main themes to be developed in the essay series.

3. Do you believe our nation was established by the "design of Providence" and that Americans at the time were "one people . . . descended from the same ancestors," as Jay (Chapter 2) contended?

4. Explain your reasons for agreeing, or not, with Hamilton's argument (Chapter 6) that commerce, far from being a pacifying influence among men and nations, only whets the appetite for wealth and power, generating rivalries conducive to strife.

5. Review Hamilton's argument (Chapter 8) about "STANDING ARMIES, and the correspondent appendages of military establishments."

6. Is politics, as Hamilton contended (Chapter 9), a "science"? Or is it the "art of the possible," as others have said? Be explicit in explaining your views.

7. Do you agree, or not, with Madison's view (Chapter 10) that the greatest source of "factions," or political parties, has always been the "various and unequal distribution of property"? Give examples in support of your opinion.

8. In what specific ways, in Hamilton's words (Chapter 11), has the United States been able "to dictate the terms" between the New World and the Old?

9. What do you think of Hamilton's pronouncement (Chapter 12) that the national government's chief source of revenue should come from "imperceptible" taxes on consumption? Is that equitable, or not? Do you favor a sales tax at any level of government? Why, or why not?

10. What is the point of Hamilton's argument (Chapter 17) that the feudal system of medieval Europe "partook of the nature" of confederacies? Is this historical analogy a sound one? Why, or why not?

11. In view of his dislike and profound distrust of the people and his confessed aversion to popular forms of government, what was Hamilton's purpose in saying (Chapter 22) that the "American Empire ought to rest on the solid basis of THE CONSENT OF THE PEOPLE"? Was this an argument against states' rights?

12. Review carefully what Hamilton set forth (Chapters 21-22) as the six major defects in the national government under the Articles of Confederation.

13. Review Hamilton's reasons for believing that, under the proposed constitution, the military could not become so strong as to dominate and even upset civilian rule, as had happened in so many countries. What, specifically, would be the checks on top American military men?

14. Has the militia system (the national guard system, as it is now called) worked out as well as Hamilton anticipated? What is its function today? Under whose command is it?

15. Do you agree, or not, with Hamilton's view that a large standing military establishment in times of relative peace and quiet is a constant menace to the people's liberties and civil rights? Be explicit in supporting your view.

16. Review Hamilton's explanation (Chapter 34) about what "concurrent jurisdiction" was and how it would operate in the field of taxation.

17. Do you believe, as Hamilton did (Chapters 35-36), that a legislature made up almost exclusively of large landowners, merchants, and lawyers could and would "truly represent" all classes and interests in the community? Be explicit in supporting your view.

18. Review Madison's argument (Chaper 39) about how the proposed new government would be at once federal and national under a "mixed Constitution."

19. Considering the Federalist arguments up to Chapter 39, do you think that the Constitutional Convention, exceeding its official instructions, was justified in drafting a whole new constitution? When, if ever, should official instructions and commissions be disobeyed?

20. Do you agree, or not, with Madison's argument (Chapter 41) that the national government should have "unlimited" power in levying taxes and borrowing money. If not, why not?

21. Review Madison's views (Chapter 42) about the slave trade.

22. What was Madison's argument (Chapter 45) to show that the "unlimited" powers to be granted to the national government would not be dangerous to the authority of the states?

23. How effective could the resistance of the states be (Chapter 46) if the national government exceeded its delegated powers?

24. What do you make of the argument (Chapters 47-48) that while separation of powers among the three main branches of government was a "sacred maxim of free government," yet such powers could not be "kept totally separate and distinct"? Why not?

25. Review the arguments (Chapters 49-51) against "occasional" or "periodical" appeals to the people to determine their views on constitutional questions.

26. Review the arguments (Chapters 52-53) in support of biennial elections to the House of Representatives.

27. What do you think of the argument (Chapter 54) that slaves, though to be counted in the general population, were to be counted as only three-fifths of a man when it came to determining how many members in the House each state was entitled to? Did this give Southern

states undue weight and influence in the House? Was this an issue in the Civil War?

28. What are the arguments for and against having the states enjoy equal representation in the Senate — two senators (two votes) for each state, regardless of wealth, size, or population? Does this give the smaller states undue weight and influence in national councils?

29. Review the explanation (Chapter 64) of why it would be desirable for the Senate to have a voice in signing foreign treaties.

30. Should the Senate have a determining voice (Chapter 66) in approving or disapproving the appointment of those chosen by the president for high government offices, such as members of his cabinet, justices of the Supreme Court, etc.?

31. List the principal powers of the president, making brief notes on the character of each and how it operates.

32. In what fields is the president restricted from acting without the advice and consent of the Senate? Do you consider such restrictions desirable, or not? Why?

33. Review Hamilton's explanation (Chapter 68) of how the electoral college would work and be composed of "men most capable" of analyzing the situation, calmly deliberating, and coming to a judicious conclusion about the candidate best qualified to become president. Has the electoral college system worked out that way? Is the college today a deliberative body with a free choice of its own, as originally envisioned?

34. What is "impeachment"? Who initiates and conducts such proceedings, and on what charges and causes? What president was impeached? What was the final disposition of the impeachment?

35. Review the argument (Chapter 78) on whether the United States Supreme Court should have the authority to declare acts of Congress null and void because "unconstitutional." Do you, or do you not, think the Supreme Court should have such authority? Explain your reasons.

36. Review the explanation (Chapter 82) of how the "doctrine of concurrent jurisdiction" between national and state courts would work.

Has it worked in practice? In general, what type of cases go to the federal courts? What type to the state and county courts?

37. Read the Constitution, especially the preamble, noting the main aims the Constitution was designed to achieve.

38. Read the first ten amendments and list the rights to which every individual American is entitled regardless of race, creed, or color. Are these rights in full effect today, some two centuries after they became the supreme law of the land? Give examples pro and con.

39. Are the Federalist papers persuasive and convincing? If you had been a voter at the time and of a divided mind about immediate ratification of the proposed constitution without prior modification or amendments, would the Hamilton-Madison-Jay arguments have made a Federalist of you? Explain why, or why not.

SELECTED BIBLIOGRAPHY

BIOGRAPHIES

Hamilton

HAMILTON, ALLAN M. *The Intimate Life of Alexander Hamilton.* New York, 1911.

LODGE, HENRY CABOT. *Alexander Hamilton* (American Statesmen series). Boston and New York, 1896.

ROSSITER, CLINTON. *Alexander Hamilton and the Constitution.* New York, 1964. This work is a scholarly, fascinating, and penetrating study by a confessed "Hamiltonian."

Madison

BRANT, IRVING. *James Madison* (5 vols.). Indianapolis, 1946-57. The chapters on Madison as "architect of the Constitution" are excellent.

GAY, SYDNEY HOWARD. *James Madison* (American Statesmen series). Boston and New York, 1896. A short and lucid book with an engaging style.

Jay

PELLEW, GEORGE. *John Jay* (in American Statesmen series). Boston and New York, 1895. While a highly polished gentleman, Jay was a dull dog, not an unusual combination.

GENERAL REFERENCES

BEARD, CHARLES A. *An Economic Interpretation of the Constitution of the United States.* New York, 1929. While some of its conclusions have been challenged as too extreme, this book opened a whole new vista on the forces that shaped the making and secured the adoption of the Constitution.

BORDEN, MORTON. *The Antifederalist Papers.* Michigan State University Press, 1965. An informative and very interesting book for special readers who wish to delve more into the subject.

BROWN, ROBERT E. *Charles Beard and the Constitution.* Princeton, 1956.

MORISON, SAMUEL ELIOT. *History of the American People.* New York, 1965. See especially Chapters 19-21.

WILLISON, GEORGE F. *Patrick Henry and His World.* New York, 1969. Read Chapters 25 and 26 on the long and bitter debate in the Virginia Constitutional Convention about ratification of the proposed constitution.

NOTES

NOTES

COREY BRUNDAGE

NOTES